Praise for *Good Questions for Math Teaching*...

This is precisely the sort of book that I go to when planning a lesson or unit. Each of these open questions gets me thinking of how I might use the task in my classrooms; many of these questions are perfect as low-stress ways to assess what students already know about a mathematical idea.

—Michael Pershan, teacher, New York City, New York, Twitter: @mpershan

Good Questions is an invaluable teaching resource. I referenced it extensively throughout my university degree. More recently, *Good Questions* has been an essential tool for supporting remote teaching. This resource is one I will use and keep forever; I highly recommend it to current and future teachers.

—Rachel McAuliffe, third-grade teacher, Victoria, Australia

The art of questioning takes practice and intuition, and the questions we ask in the course of a lesson have the potential to lower or raise the cognitive demand of a task. With *Good Questions*, math educators learn how to craft artful questions that help students delve deeper into mathematical concepts. Readers are provided with numerous examples of good questions, as well as the features that are specific to good questions so that they can learn to develop their own repertoire of good questions. A must-read for any math educator seeking to create a dynamic learning environment for their students.

—Mary Shapiro, instructional math coach, Milton Public Schools, Milton, Massachusetts

Questioning lies at the heart of good instruction. Every professional learning developer, coach, teacher, and teacher educator should have a copy of this resource close at hand.

—Mary Kay Stein, Professor, University of Pittsburgh, Pennsylvania

Good Questions is a wonderful resource for teachers. All teachers ask questions; however, this resource provides them with open-ended questions that will spark discussion and will force students to think deeply about the mathematics. All discussions start with a good question, and this book has plenty!

—Suzanne H. Chapin, coauthor of Talk Moves: A Teacher's Guide for Using Classroom Discussions in Math, Third Edition

This series does a great job of reminding us that good questions allow students to be creative and innovative, highlighting different strengths that would be otherwise ignored.

—Gregory Benoit, Assistant Director of the Earl Center, Lecturer Mathematics Education, Boston University Wheelock College of Education, Boston, Massachusetts

As a math teacher, I supplement my curriculum to encourage my students to explore various topics and develop deeper comprehension. *Good Questions* helps me do that while addressing the needs of my wide range of students. For example, while working on a ratios unit, I ask questions to extend some of my students' thinking while other students continue to make connections to prior knowledge. *Good Questions* gives you the context behind what good questions are, how to create them, and meaningful ways to apply the questions to your planning.

—*Doana Marcellus, teacher, Milton Academy, Milton, Massachusetts*

Math teachers are always on the lookout for great questions to ask their students—questions that offer the right amount of challenge, that can be approached in multiple ways, and that allow teachers the opportunity to assess what students know. *Good Questions* is a wonderful resource for exactly these kinds of questions. *Good Questions* is packed with excellent questions from a wide range of content domains and can be used in conjunction with any curriculum. It is definitely worth a look!

—*Jon R. Star, Professor of Education, Harvard Graduate School of Education, Boston, Massachusetts*

Teachers are often looking for ways to open up their questions but may not be quite clear on how to do so. This series provides excellent guidance, with a very clear explanation of the four main features of good questions and many immediately usable examples. New teachers will use this resource to learn what good questions are, and veteran teachers will use it to create and refine their own good questions. I know I will use it in my work with future teachers as well as students!

—*Julie McNamara, coauthor of* Beyond Pizzas and Pies: 10 Essential Strategies for Supporting Fraction Sense, Second Edition

Good Questions is a practical resource that teaches math educators how to design and ask questions that encourage students to be challenged, to solve problems, and to think deeply about mathematics.

—*Jin Lee, math teacher, Milton Academy, Milton, Massachusetts*

As a vocational adult education trainer and assessor, I have found the *Good Questions* series to be an invaluable resource for developing the problem-solving skills of supervisors and managers. *Good Questions* provides excellent examples of the questioning skills that enable supervisors and managers to be confident that their staff and teams actually understand the underlying requirements of the required task.

—*Mike Stoll, MBA, DIP Training and Assessment, Victoria, Australia*

GRADES 5–8

Good Questions for Math Teaching
Why Ask Them and What to Ask

SECOND EDITION

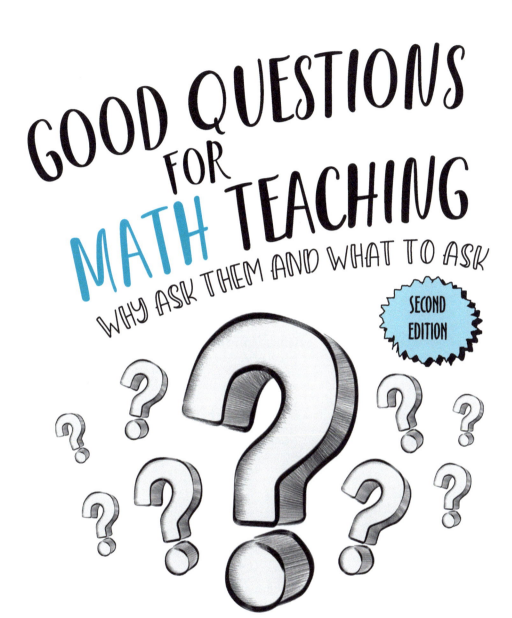

LAINIE SCHUSTER · NANCY ANDERSON
Series Editor, Nancy Anderson

HEINEMANN
Portsmouth, NH

Heinemann
145 Maplewood Avenue, Suite 300
Portsmouth, NH 03801
www.heinemann.com

Copyright © 2020 by Heinemann

Good Questions for Math Teaching, Grades 5–8, Second Edition was originally published by Houghton Mifflin Harcourt under the Math Solutions brand, ISBN: 978-1-935099-77-2.

All rights reserved, including but not limited to the right to reproduce this book, or portions thereof, in any form or by any means whatsoever, without written permission from the publisher. For information on permission for reproductions or subsidiary rights licensing, please contact Heinemann at permissions@heinemann.com.

Heinemann's authors have dedicated their entire careers to developing the unique content in their works, and their written expression is protected by copyright law. We respectfully ask that you do not adapt, reuse, or copy anything on third-party (whether for-profit or not-for-profit) lesson-sharing websites.

—Heinemann Publishers

"Dedicated to Teachers" is a trademark of Greenwood Publishing Group, LLC.

Cataloging-in-Publication data is on file with the Library of Congress.

ISBN-13: 978-0-325-13760-5
eISBN-13: 978-0-325-13942-5

Executive Editor: Jamie Ann Cross
Production Manager: Denise A. Botelho
Editorial Assistant: Kirby Sandmeyer
Interior Design and Composition: Publishers' Design and Production Services, Inc.
Photo Credits: Lainie Schuster by Lainie Schuster; Nancy Anderson by Portrait Simple
Cover Design: Susan Olinsky Design
Manufacturing: Gerard Clancy
Cover Art: Question mark art created by sdecoret / Shutterstock

Printed in the United States of America on acid-free paper.
1 2 3 4 5   GP   26 25 24 23 22   PO34840

A Message from Heinemann

Heinemann's math professional resources are written by educators, for educators, to support student-centered teaching and learning. Our authors provide classroom-tested guidance, advice, and proven best practices to help teachers increase their comfort and confidence with teaching math. We believe a focus on reasoning and understanding is the pathway to helping students make sense of the mathematics they're learning.

This resource was originally published by Math Solutions, a company long dedicated to similar ideals and aims as Heinemann. In 2022, Math Solutions Publications became part of Heinemann. While the logo on the cover is different, the heart of Math Solutions lives in these pages: that teaching math well calls for increasing our understanding of the math we teach, seeking deeper insights into how students learn mathematics, and refining our lessons to best promote students' learning.

To learn more about our resources and authors, please visit Heinemann.com/Math.

Brief Contents

List of Reproducibles		xiii
Acknowledgments		xv
How to Use This Resource		xvii
Why This Resource?		xvii
How Is This Resource Organized?		xviii
When Should I Use These Questions?		xviii

PART I	**The Importance of Good Questions**		**1**
CHAPTER 1	What Are Good Questions?		3
CHAPTER 2	How Do I Create Good Questions?		9
CHAPTER 3	Five Steps to Successfully Implementing Good Questions in Your Classroom		13
PART II	**Good Questions to Use in Math Lessons**		**21**
CHAPTER 4	Good Questions for Number Relationships		23
CHAPTER 5	Good Questions for Multiplication and Proportional Reasoning		53
CHAPTER 6	Good Questions for Fractions, Decimals, and Percentages		79
CHAPTER 7	Good Questions for Geometry		133

(Continued)

CHAPTER 8	Good Questions for Algebraic Thinking	157
CHAPTER 9	Good Questions for Data Analysis and Probability	199
CHAPTER 10	Good Questions for Measurement	231

| Reproducibles | 277 |
| References | 313 |

How to Access Online Resources

To access the downloadable reproducibles referenced in the text, please see page xx for directions, visit http://hein.pub/MathOLR, and register for an account. Use key code GQ58 to register this product and download.

Contents

List of Reproducibles		xiii
Acknowledgments		xv
How to Use This Resource		xvii
Why This Resource?		xvii
How Is This Resource Organized?		xviii
When Should I Use These Questions?		xviii

PART I	**The Importance of Good Questions**	**1**
CHAPTER 1	What Are Good Questions?	3
CHAPTER 2	How Do I Create Good Questions?	9
CHAPTER 3	Five Steps to Successfully Implementing Good Questions in Your Classroom	13

PART II	**Good Questions to Use in Math Lessons**	**21**
CHAPTER 4	Good Questions for Number Relationships	23
	Grades 5–6	24
	Factors and Multiples	24
	Even and Odd	30
	Polygonal Numbers	35
	Integers	39

(Continued)

	Grades 7–8	42
	Number Relationships	42
CHAPTER 5	Good Questions for Multiplication and Proportional Reasoning	53
	Grades 5–6	54
	Multiplication and Proportional Reasoning	54
	Grades 7–8	70
	Multiplication and Proportional Reasoning	70
CHAPTER 6	Good Questions for Fractions, Decimals, and Percentages	79
	Grades 5–6	81
	Fractions	81
	Decimals	99
	Percentages	110
	Grades 7–8	115
	Fractions	115
	Decimals	121
	Percentages	126
CHAPTER 7	Good Questions for Geometry	133
	Grades 5–6	134
	Two-Dimensional Shapes	134
	Grades 7–8	147
	Two-Dimensional Shapes	147
	Three-Dimensional Shapes	153
CHAPTER 8	Good Questions for Algebraic Thinking	157
	Grades 5–6	158
	Algebraic Thinking	158
	Grades 7–8	184
	Algebraic Thinking	184
CHAPTER 9	Good Questions for Data Analysis and Probability	199
	Grades 5–6	200
	Data Analysis	200
	Probability	208
	Grades 7–8	216
	Data Analysis	216
	Probability	223

CHAPTER 10	Good Questions for Measurement	231
	Grades 5–6	232
	Temperature, Time, and Length	232
	Weight	235
	Area and Perimeter	240
	Volume	250
	Grades 7–8	257
	Weight	257
	Area	261
	Length and Perimeter	265
	Volume and Capacity	271

Reproducibles	277
References	313

How to Access Online Resources

To access the downloadable reproducibles referenced in the text, please see page xx for directions, visit http://hein.pub/MathOLR, and register for an account. Use key code **GQ58** to register this product and download.

Reproducibles

The following reproducibles are referenced throughout the text. These reproducibles are also available in a downloadable, printable format. For access, visit http://hein.pub/MathOLR and register your product using the key code **GQ58**. See page xx for more detailed instructions.

Reproducible 1	Fair Game 2
Reproducible 2	Pattern Block Figure
Reproducible 3	Grid Figure
Reproducible 4	Fractions Dot Paper
Reproducible 5	6-by-6-Inch Template
Reproducible 6	Tenths and Hundredths Grids
Reproducible 7	Hundredths Grid
Reproducible 8	∠HAT
Reproducible 9	Clock Faces
Reproducible 10	Polygon Sets
Reproducible 11	Polygon Venn Diagram and Shape Bank
Reproducible 12	Polygon Venn Diagram (Extension)

(Continued)

xiii

(Continued)

Reproducible 13	Rectangle ABCD
Reproducible 14	Number Path A
Reproducible 15	Number Path B
Reproducible 16	Patio Borders
Reproducible 17	Pencil Sharpener Stories and Graphs
Reproducible 18	As Time Goes by Graphs
Reproducible 19	Grouping Patterns
Reproducible 20	Walk-a-Thon Graphs
Reproducible 21	Perimeter and Area Tables
Reproducible 22	Mystery Line Plots
Reproducible 23	Investment Graphs
Reproducible 24	Dart Board
Reproducible 25	Bags of Marbles
Reproducible 26	Weights
Reproducible 27	Irregular Polygon
Reproducible 28	Cutout Polygon Models
Reproducible 29	Volume Pattern
Reproducible 30	Prisms
Reproducible A	Graph Paper
Reproducible B	Dot Paper
Reproducible C	Blank Spinner Faces

Acknowledgments

Peter Sullivan and Pat Lilburn's *Good Questions for Math Teaching: Why Ask Them and What to Ask, K–5, Second Edition* (2020) has been the model for much of our work in this book. Sullivan and Lilburn's book has been extremely popular with teachers because of its content, format, and user-friendliness. We hope our book will complement theirs.

We teach in an era of wonderful resources and standards-based curricula. Our teaching has continued to develop and improve because of them. We would like to acknowledge the following series, publications, and their authors, from which we adapted many of our questions: *Everyday Mathematics* (The University of Chicago, 2002); *Math Matters, Second Edition* (Math Solutions, 2006); the Connected Mathematics Project series (Michigan State University, 2002); the Hot Math Topics series (Dale Seymour Publications, 2001), and the Investigations in Number, Data, and Space series (Scott Foresman, 2004).

We would like to thank all the teachers who used the first edition of this book in their instruction. Your honest feedback and effusive praise contributed to the new edition here. We hope we have kept all of the questions that you told us you loved and provided you with some new ones too!

We both have been extremely fortunate to have had opportunities to work with Dr. Suzanne Chapin. Her influence on our professional lives has been enormous. Suzanne is a colleague, a teacher, a mentor, and a wonderful friend.

We cannot think of any one person who has more influenced the teaching of mathematics than Marilyn Burns. Marilyn's vision and passion for thinking mathematically are what push us to ask the "good" questions.

We would also like to give special thanks to our editor, Jamie Cross, as well as our editorial assistant, Kirby Sandmeyer, and Denise Botelho and her production team. We appreciate their patience, "gentle nudges," and skill guiding this project along the way.

It is our students, however, who continue to inspire, motivate, and surprise us. This book is written for them.

—Lainie Schuster and Nancy Anderson

How to Use This Resource

Why This Resource?

Our goals of education are for our students to think, to learn, to analyze, to criticize, and to be able to solve unfamiliar problems, and it follows that good questions should be part of the instructional repertoire of all teachers of mathematics. As we work to emphasize problem solving, application of concepts and procedures, and the development of a variety of thinking skills in our mathematics curricula, it becomes vital that we pay increased attention to the improvement of our questioning techniques in mathematics lessons. As teachers of mathematics, we want our students not only to understand what they think but also to be able to articulate how they arrived at those understandings. Developing productive questions can help focus learning on the process of thinking while attending to the study of content (Dantonio and Beisenherz 2001, 60). Good questions created and posed by teachers ultimately become powerful tools for student learning.

In *Good Questions for Math Teaching, Grades 5–8, Second Edition*, we describe the features of good questions, show how to create good questions, give some practical ideas for using them in your classroom, and provide many good questions that you can use in your mathematics program. By asking careful, purposeful questions, teachers create dynamic learning environments, help students make sense of math, and unravel misconceptions.

xvii

How Is This Resource Organized?

This resource is divided into two parts: Part I: "The Importance of Good Questions," and Part II: "Good Questions to Use in Math Lessons."

Part I

In Part I, we explain what we mean by "good questions," walk you through different methods to create your own good questions, and provide necessary support for how to use good questions in your classroom.

Part II

In Part II, we offer examples of good questions, broken down by topic and grade level, for you to select from and use in your classroom. Each question is accompanied by notes to support your teaching.

When Should I Use These Questions?

Here are a few of our favorite scenarios for when to use good questions.

When to Use Good Questions

- Use good questions to supplement your mathematics curriculum.
- Use good questions for warm-up routines or for review.
- Incorporate good questions into homework and/or assessments.

Use Good Questions to Supplement Your Mathematics Curriculum

The questions in this book are designed as a supplement to your mathematics curriculum. Good questions can be used as the basis for an entire lesson, either as a lesson that stands alone or as part of a unit of study. As you progress through a unit of study, you may want to ask your students questions in this book that correspond to that unit. Embedding questions from this book in your lessons may further enhance student learning and understanding. When studying ratios, for example, you may wish to refer to the questions in this book to support, extend, or enrich your present curriculum. If current practice has your students solving word problems that have only one answer, you may wish to ask students questions that allow for multiple answers—and approaches—such as Question 1 on page 71: *A vase holds red and white roses only. There are 1.5 times as many red roses as white roses. How many flowers might be in the vase?* By constructing an answer to this question, students gain valuable experience with ratio and also gain insights into the relationship between ratios and multiplicative reasoning.

Use Good Questions for Warm-Up Routines or for Review

Another way to use this book is to use the questions as a daily warm-up activity or "do now" activity for the start of math class. You may choose a question that corresponds to the current unit or a question that requires students to review a particularly challenging or important skill or concept. Students can talk about the question with their peers before you bring everyone together for a whole-class discussion. This routine makes good use of transition time while immediately focusing math class on reasoning and communication.

Incorporate Good Questions into Homework and/or Assessments

In addition to using these questions during instructional time, you could assign them for homework or incorporate them into your assessments. Typically, math homework and assessment practices tend to focus on skills and/or closed questions that require recall of what was learned in class. If your students usually complete a review worksheet of the day's lesson, attach (or even substitute) a question from this book that will require them to think beyond what they have learned, to connect an understanding from a previous lesson, or to confront a misconception that may have arisen during class. In addition, if students' assessments normally include computations and problems for which there is only one correct answer, adapt those assessments to include some questions from this book that will allow students to think creatively about the mathematics they are learning.

HOW TO USE THIS RESOURCE   xix

How to Access Online Resources

1. Go to http://hein.pub/MathOLR and log in if you already have an account. If you do not, click or tap the Create New Account button at the bottom of the Log In form.
2. Create an account. You will receive a confirmation email when your account has been created.
3. Once your account has been created, you will be taken to the Product Registration page. Click Register on the product you would like to access (in this case, *Good Questions for Math Teaching, Grades 5–8, Second Edition*).
4. Enter key code **GQ58** and click or tap the Submit Key Code button.
5. Click or tap the Complete Registration button.
6. To access the reproducibles at any time, visit your account page.

[Key Code GQ58]

More Resources in This Series!

We are excited to share this resource, *Good Questions for Math Teaching, Grades K–5, Second Edition*, as one of several resources in the Good Questions series. For more titles, see Heinemann.com/Math.

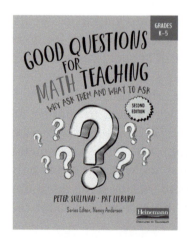

Grades K–5
ISBN: 978-0-325-13759-9

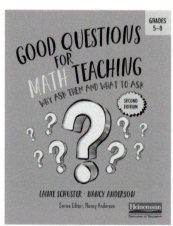

Grades 5–8
ISBN: 978-0-325-13760-5

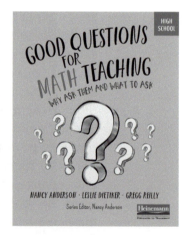

High School
ISBN: 978-0-325-16026-9

PART I

THE IMPORTANCE OF GOOD QUESTIONS

CHAPTER 1   What Are Good Questions?   3

CHAPTER 2   How Do I Create Good Questions?   9

CHAPTER 3   Five Steps to Successfully Implementing Good Questions in Your Classroom   13

In Part I, we explain what we mean by good questions, walk you through different methods to create your own good questions, and provide necessary support for how to use good questions in your classroom. Remember, the power of questioning is ultimately in the answering. As teachers, we not only need to ask good questions to get good answers but need to ask good questions to promote the thinking required to give good answers.

CHAPTER 1

WHAT ARE GOOD QUESTIONS?

During the course of a normal school day teachers ask many questions. In fact, something like 60 percent of the things said by teachers are questions and most of these are not planned. One way of categorizing questions is to describe them as either open or closed. Closed questions are those that simply require an answer or a response to be given from memory, such as a description of a situation or object or the reproduction of a skill. Open questions are those that require a student to think more deeply and to give a response that involves more than recalling a fact or reproducing a skill.

Teachers are usually skilled at asking open questions in content areas such as language arts or social studies. For example, teachers often ask students to interpret situations or justify opinions. However, in mathematics lessons closed questions are much more common.

Questions that encourage students to do more than recall known facts have the potential to stimulate thinking and reasoning. To emphasize problem solving, application, and the development of a variety of thinking skills it is vital that we pay more attention to improving our questioning in mathematics lessons. Teachers should use questions that develop their students' higher levels of thinking.

Good Questions for Math Teaching, Grades 5–8, looks in more detail at a particular type of open question that we call a "good" question. Good questions can set the stage for meaningful classroom discussion and learning. When we ask good questions in math class, we invite our students to think, to understand, and to share a mathematical journey with their classmates and teachers alike. Students are no longer passive receivers of information when asked questions that challenge their understandings and convictions about mathematics. They become active and engaged in the construction of their own mathematical understanding and knowledge.

Careful, intentional, and mindful questioning is one of the most powerful tools a skillful teacher possesses (Costa and Kallick 2000,

34). So, what do good questions "look" like? Let's consider four main features.

Four Main Features of Good Questions

1. Good questions help students make sense of the mathematics.
2. Students can learn by answering good questions, and the teacher learns about each student from the attempt.
3. Good questions may have several acceptable answers.
4. Good questions are accessible to all students.

FEATURE 1: GOOD QUESTIONS HELP STUDENTS MAKE SENSE OF THE MATHEMATICS

Too often mathematics is presented in a closed or rote manner: students are given a procedure (or told about a concept) and then asked to absorb that information without much reflection or exploration. Good questions, on the other hand, require more than remembering a fact or reproducing a skill. Their open-endedness requires the application of facts and procedures while simultaneously encouraging students to make connections and generalizations. Good questions help students see mathematics as a subject that is based on sense making. In turn, good questions empower students to think of themselves as capable sense makers. Let's look at a couple scenarios to help further explore this.

Scenario 1: Part-to-Part Ratio Questions

Think about the following two questions—which one do you feel is more powerful in helping a student make sense of mathematics? Why?

Question A: *A vase holds red and white roses only. There are 3 red roses and 2 white roses. What is the ratio of red to white roses?*

Question B: *A vase holds red and white roses only. There are 1.5 times as many red roses as white roses. How many flowers might be in the vase?*

Question A might be considered the typical kind of part-to-part ratio question that is asked of students in the middle grades. These questions typically present students with information about two quantities and ask them to express this information as a ratio. While we would not want these questions to disappear entirely, we also recognize that these questions have their limitations. Specifically, they do not empower students to make decisions based on what makes sense or consider connections between important mathematical concepts. What if we took Question A and opened it up? That's where Question B—what we consider a "good question"—comes into play. Question B invites students to dig deeply into the multiplicative relationship between the values in a ratio while also making decisions about how to organize their thinking and find more than one possible answer. By opening up the question, we empower students to think of themselves as capable sense makers. When students are given many opportunities to derive their own strategies, try them out, make adjustments, and justify their reasoning, they gain knowledge, thinking skills, and confidence. And when students are exposed to a classroom environment where good questions are the norm, something else wonderful happens too. The "let's try it and see what happens" thinking at the heart of any good question motivates students to generate their own good questions! In Question B, since there is a range of acceptable answers (e.g., 3 red and 2 white, 9 red and 6 white, 30 red and 20 white), students might wonder:

- What is a generalization about all possible answers?
- How might my strategy or approach change if the givens of the problem changed—say there were two-thirds as many red roses as white roses?

The nature of the question stimulates students' natural sense of curiosity, which in turn fosters the higher-level thinking and the problem-solving skills that are essential to the work of doing mathematics in school and beyond.

Scenario 2: Measurement

Here's one more example of the power of a good question. Yolanda, a seventh grader, had just finished a unit on two-dimensional measurement where she had been asked to find the measures of attributes of polygons and circles. She was able to complete most of these correctly, and the teacher assumed from this that Yolanda could use measurement formulas and the relationships between attributes of a shape to solve a variety of problems. With this in mind, the teacher gave Yolanda the following good question:

A round banquet table seats 10 people comfortably. What might be the diameter (in feet) of this table?

Yolanda read this question several times and, exasperated, responded, "I can't do this! There isn't enough information." What happened?

To find an answer, Yolanda needed to think about the relationship between the circumference of the table and its diameter. She needed to use higher-order reasoning skills and estimation since she had to consider the length of table that might be needed for one person to sit at the table. This certainly required her to do more than remember a fact or reproduce a skill. It required higher-order reasoning skills including comprehension of the task, application of the concepts and appropriate skills, and analysis and some synthesis of the major concepts involved. Through further probing, this question allowed the teacher to see that Yolanda had little appreciation for the meaning of circumference as the length of the circle or the relationship between circumference and diameter. She had learned to answer routine story problems without fully understanding the concepts.

Feature 2: Students Can Learn by Answering Good Questions, and the Teacher Learns about Each Student from the Attempt

Good questions have the potential to make students more aware of what they do know and what they do not know. That is, students can become aware of where their understanding is incomplete as well as where they have developed misunderstandings. Let's revisit the earlier question from Scenario 1:

A vase holds red and white roses only. There are 1.5 times as many red roses as white roses. How many flowers might be in the vase?

The very act of trying to answer the question can help students gain a better understanding of the concepts involved. Imagine that a group of students told their teacher that the problem doesn't make sense because there is no such thing as 1.5 flowers. By answering this question, the students and their teacher both learn about their current level of understanding of ratios. The students understand that the measures of ratios are often whole numbers and that the values in a problem should fit the given context. This is encouraging! However, in this problem, they have confounded the multiplicative relationship between the measures in a ratio with the measures themselves. With this revelation, the students and their teacher can now work toward helping them reach a deeper level of understanding so that the students can find whole number values that have a multiplicative factor equal to 1.5. Use of the good question not only reveals misconceptions to the teacher (proving to be a valuable assessment tool) but also can empower the students to use their mistakes as learning tools.

Feature 3: Good Questions May Have Several Acceptable Answers

Many of the questions teachers ask, especially during mathematics lessons, have only one correct answer. Such questions are acceptable, but there are many other questions that are open-ended, allowing multiple answers, and teachers should make a point of asking these, too. Each of the good questions that we have already looked at has several possible answers. Because of this, these questions foster higher-level thinking, encouraging students to develop their problem-solving expertise at the same time as they are acquiring mathematical skills. Good questions also dispel the myth that math problems always have just one right answer.

Feature 4: Good Questions Are Accessible to All Students

Good questions invite all students into the conversation. Because good questions allow for multiple entry points, students can use their prior knowledge as a gateway toward new understandings. Take, for example, the earlier question on ratios:

A vase holds red and white roses only. There are 1.5 times as many red roses as white roses. How many flowers might be in the vase?

Some students may access this question by making a sketch while others may rely on ratio tables or equivalent ratios. Because this question has multiple answers, it supports students with emerging, developing, or advanced understanding of multiplicative reasoning and ratios. Good questions are accessible to all students because they do not require only one set pathway or approach.

Looking Ahead

In this chapter, we have looked more closely at the four main features that categorize good questions. The next chapter shares two ways to construct your own good questions.

CHAPTER 2

How Do I Create Good Questions?

When you first start using good questions, we suggest you select your questions from the collection of questions in Part II, "Good Questions to Use in Math Lessons." After a while you will want to create good questions for yourself. Detailed in this chapter are two methods that can be used to create good questions. The one you use is a matter of personal preference.

Two Methods for Creating Good Questions

1. Working Backward
2. Modifying a Standard Question

When creating your own good questions, it's important to plan the questions in advance, because creating them is not something that can be done in the moment. Creating good questions relies heavily on the destination we have in mind. What do we expect our students to be able to do, say, or understand by the end of the lesson? Beginning with the end in mind requires us to start with a clear understanding of desired knowledge, learning, and outcomes. When we think about questions that we might ask our students, it is helpful to first ask ourselves a few questions; for example:

- What are the mathematical goals of the lesson?
- What are the connections we'd like students to make between lesson goals and previously covered concepts and/or procedures?
- What are the misconceptions students may have?
- What is our assessment of students' understanding?

9

METHOD 1: WORKING BACKWARD

This method is a three-step process.

The Working Backward Method

Step 1. Identify a topic.
Step 2. Think of a closed question and write down the answer.
Step 3. Make up a question that includes (or addresses) the answer.

For example:

Step 1. The topic for tomorrow is circumference of circles.
Step 2. The closed question might be *Find the circumference of a circle with a diameter of 6 feet.*
Step 3. The good question could be *A round banquet table seats 10 people comfortably. What might be the diameter (in feet) of this table?*

Some more examples of how this works are shown in the following table.

STEP 1 Identify a topic.	STEP 2 Think of a closed question and write down the answer.	STEP 3 Make up a question that includes (or addresses) the answer.
simplifying expressions	$2 - 4x$	Write three other expressions that are equivalent to the expression $6 - 4(x + 1)$.
irrational numbers	$\sqrt{2}$ inches	Create a square on a geoboard with an area that is not a square number. How long is each side of your square?
perimeter	The side lengths of a triangle are $3\frac{1}{2}$, 7, and $8\frac{1}{4}$ inches.	What might be the side lengths of a triangle with a perimeter of $18\frac{3}{4}$ inches?

(Continued)

STEP 1 Identify a topic.	STEP 2 Think of a closed question and write down the answer.	STEP 3 Make up a question that includes (or addresses) the answer.
data	In a recent survey, 137 out of 200 people said they participate in voluntary recycling. Write this statement as a percent.	In a recent survey, 0.685 of the people surveyed said they participate in voluntary recycling. Write an attention-grabbing headline about this statement.

Method 2: Modifying a Standard Question

This is also a three-step process.

The Modifying a Standard Question Method

Step 1. Identify a topic.
Step 2. Think of a standard question.
Step 3. Modify it to make a good question.

For example:

Step 1.   The topic for tomorrow is ratios.
Step 2.   A typical exercise might be *A vase holds red and white roses only. There are 3 red roses and 2 white roses. What is the ratio of red to white roses?* (The answer is 3 to 2.)
Step 3.   The good question could be *A vase holds red and white roses only. There are 1.5 times as many red roses as white roses. How many flowers might be in the vase?*

Some more examples of how this works are shown in the following table.

GOOD QUESTIONS FOR MATH TEACHING   11

STEP 1 Identify a topic.	STEP 2 Think of a standard question.	STEP 3 Modify it to make a good question.
fractions	Write in order from least to greatest: $\frac{1}{2}$, $\frac{3}{7}$, $\frac{2}{5}$, $\frac{5}{8}$	Use some of the digits 2, 3, 4, 5, 6, 7, and 8 to create fractions that could replace the missing values in the inequality. $? < ? < \frac{1}{2} < ?$
decimals	Is the product of 1.6×1.7 greater than or less than the factors?	Can you create a problem in which the product of two decimals is larger than either of the numbers multiplied? What was your strategy?
integers	Find the product of $-6 \times 2 \times 4$	Mannie multiplied three integers and got a product of -48. What might the integers have been?
three-dimensional shapes	How many cubes make up the prism?	I have a rectangular prism made up of interlocking cubes. Twenty cubes have exactly two faces showing. How many cubes might be in the prism?

Looking Ahead

The more experience you have with good questions, the more you will want to use them, and the easier it will become for you to make up your own. Refer to either or both of the methods outlined in this chapter to help you feel confident in creating your own (in doing so, you might also "invent" additional methods!). In the next chapter, we outline five steps to successfully implementing good questions in your classroom.

CHAPTER 3

Five Steps to Successfully Implementing Good Questions in Your Classroom

Today's mathematics classrooms should be dynamic places where students are involved and engaged in their own learning. This can be achieved through activities that promote higher-level thinking, cooperative problem solving, and communication. We have seen that good questions support these activities and are readily available for teachers to use. But how can you ensure success with good questions? In this chapter we outline five steps we've found helpful in successfully implementing good questions, including advice for overcoming problems that might arise at each stage. We then take you through each of the steps using a specific good question.

Five Steps to Successfully Implementing Good Questions

1. Prepare the good question.
2. Present the good question.
3. Students work on the good question.
4. Facilitate a whole-class discussion.
5. Summarize.

Step 1: Prepare the Good Question

See Chapters 1 and 2 for guidance in understanding what makes up a good question as well as how to create good questions. Remember that

Part II of this resource offers many classroom-tested good questions for you to select and use as well.

Once you've selected a good question, it's critical that you understand the mathematics embedded in the question. On your own or with colleagues, think through the question and solve it. This is of particular importance with good questions because they might have more than one answer and/or approach. Try to think of more than just one answer. Doing so will help you anticipate and then react to the variety of responses you will hear from your students (undoubtedly, students will think of things you did not!). Remember, working through good mathematics takes time. An understanding of the mathematics involved in the question will help you determine the amount of time students might need to process and answer it.

Make sure the question is appropriate for your students; consider how students may begin the process of answering it. If needed, adjust the language and/or add more data to a question to ensure accessibility for all. Following are questions we've found helpful in working through a good question prior to teaching with it.

Questions for Preparing a Good Question

- Do I have the necessary materials (e.g., graph paper, chart paper, manipulatives)? If not, where can I get them?
- What misconceptions or difficulties might my students have with the language, concepts, or directions?
- What follow-up questions can I ask that will readdress or redirect misconceptions or difficulties?
- How much time will students need to answer the question?

STEP 2: PRESENT THE GOOD QUESTION

When presenting the good question to students, write it on the board where everyone can see it. As you ask the question, refer to the corresponding words on the board. Make sure that all students know what the question is; do not assume they know just because they can see it. Consider asking some students to repeat the question in their own words.

Allow time for students to ask you about the meaning of the question. Clarify the question to them if necessary but do not give any directions or suggestions on how to do it. This is for students to work out for themselves. The following is a summary of essentials we like to revisit before presenting good questions.

Essentials for Presenting Good Questions

- Present the question clearly using accessible mathematical language.
- Set clear and reasonable expectations for student work.
- Allow for individual approaches, methods, and/or answers.
- Ensure concrete materials are available for student use.

Step 3: Students Work on the Good Question

Once the question has been introduced, allow ample time for student investigation. We suggest having students work in pairs or small groups. This gives them the opportunity to communicate their ideas to others. Not only do students hear and learn from one another's answers, they also rehearse their thinking before sharing with the whole class (we've found that students are often more willing to share their reasoning and ideas with the whole class once they have first had a chance to practice with a small group). Encourage students to keep written records of their thinking together—calculations, charts, diagrams, and/or pictures. This documentation will help them support and defend their thinking and answers.

Pair or small-group work can also benefit students who may have difficulty starting. Students should be encouraged to go to each other first before seeking help from the teacher. Suggest that they try representing the problem in some way, such as by drawing a diagram or using materials (a variety of concrete materials should always be available for students to reference).

If, as students are working, you find that there are too many who cannot make progress without your assistance, you might need to reconvene as a class. Have students share their concerns. If the concerns of each group—or individuals within each group—are all different, then this is a sign that the question you have posed may need to be further

GOOD QUESTIONS FOR MATH TEACHING   **15**

modified. You could also decide to abandon the question altogether as unsuitable at this stage. If this happens, do not worry, because it takes time and practice to choose appropriate good questions. We assure you it's worth the effort and perseverance.

Once students are working, monitor their progress and note strategies, partial understandings, and misconceptions. If students stop after giving one response, ask them to look for other possible answers. If they have found all possible answers, ask them to explain their thinking behind each answer. You could also ask a related question to extend their learning. For example, you could change the parameters of the problem, add an additional step, or change the size of the numbers in the problem.

Step 4: Facilitate a Whole-Class Discussion

Facilitate a whole-class sharing of answers, strategies, and the discovered mathematics. This is a meaningful time for students to reflect and build on their learning. Class discussions offer opportunities for students to achieve understanding by processing information, applying reasoning, hearing ideas from others, and connecting new thinking to what they already know (Chapin, O'Connor, and Anderson 2013).

You do not have to wait until *all* groups have finished the task before initiating a discussion; it is better to stop while students are still engaged with the question and interested in the task. Consider signaling to groups that they have five minutes left before the whole-class discussion.

As students share, write their responses where everyone can see them and/or display their visual representation. If there are errors, work together to identify such and figure out why. Often, as students are explaining their work, they discover the error themselves.

Guide the conversation by keeping the focus on students' thinking. Encourage students to support, add to, and even disagree with one another's strategies. Have them address one another, not you. The following questions may help guide and facilitate discussions of students' answers.

> ### Questions to Prompt Whole-Class Discussions
>
> - Why do you think that?
> - How did you know to try that strategy?
> - How do you know you have an answer?
> - Will this work with every number? Every similar situation?
> - When will this strategy not work? What is a counterexample?
> - Who has a different strategy?
> - How is your answer similar to or different from another student's answer?
> - Repeat your classmate's ideas in your own words.
> - Do you agree or disagree with your classmate's idea? Why?

STEP 5: SUMMARIZE

Typically, a summary of the main learning will naturally evolve as the whole-class discussion does. Continually check for understanding; just because a few students are eager to share does not mean everyone understands. To wrap up, review key points with everyone. Reference visual representations and use teaching aids as needed to support the needs of your students. Relate the answers back to the question. It is also helpful to pose more questions using a similar format so that students can apply what they have learned to new situations.

THE FIVE STEPS IN ACTION

Let's have a look at how the five steps might unfold in a seventh-grade classroom.

Step 1: Prepare the Good Question

Ms. Garcia wants a question to supplement the unit on multiplication and proportional reasoning that her students are learning. She selects the following question and solves it. With colleagues, she identifies possible misconceptions and difficulties she feels students may have including confusion about how non-integer values can be used to compare measures within a ratio. She notes to ask follow-up questions to guide

GOOD QUESTIONS FOR MATH TEACHING   17

and redirect (e.g., "What does 1.5 times as many" mean? How is a comparison like this similar to the comparison "three times as many"? How is it different?). She might also suggest that students use counters to represent the roses. She notes that, if needed, she can make the question easier by changing the comparison statement to a whole number (e.g., There are 3 times as many red roses as white roses). Based on this preliminary work, she decides to allow approximately five minutes for students to investigate the question.

The Good Question

A vase holds red and white roses only. There are 1.5 times as many red roses as white roses. How many flowers might be in the vase?

Step 2: Present the Good Question

Ms. Garcia writes the question on the board where all students can see it. She asks some students to read the question out loud and asks others to tell her what it means in their own words. She gives time for students to ask questions, being careful not to give any directions or suggestions on how to do the task.

Step 3: Students Work on the Good Question

Ms. Garcia has students work on the question in small groups. She circulates and observes. One group stops after discovering one response. She encourages the group to look for other possible answers. Several other groups find a few answers; she asks them to think of a way to describe all their answers—is there a pattern or a rule? What is it? For one group that finishes more quickly than the others, she prompts them to form the generalization that any ratio equivalent to 3 red to 2 white flowers is a possible answer to the question.

When all groups have at least one response to the question, Ms. Garcia gives them a heads-up that they have five minutes before the whole-class discussion. She is OK with groups being at different stages in their work.

Step 4: Facilitate a Whole-Class Discussion

Ms. Garcia brings everyone together for a whole-class discussion. She asks students to share their answers. The answers from three different groups are:

- Group B: *The problem can't be solved; you can't have half a rose.*
- Group E: *3 red and 2 white*
- Group C: *It could be 3 red to 2 white, 6 red to 4 white, 30 red to 20 white, or any ratio equivalent to 3:2.*

Ms. Garcia notes that these three responses differ not only in the level of mathematical understanding but also in the quality of thinking that is demonstrated by the answers. She takes a positive approach to each group's response. She asks Group B to interpret the statement "half as many" and use this to think again about the statement "one and a half times as many." She asks Group E to find at least one more possible answer. She has Group C organize their answers in a table and describe the patterns they see. She continually encourages discussion using questions like:

- "Why do you think that?"
- "How is your answer similar to or different from another student's answer?"
- "Do you agree or disagree with your classmate's idea? Why?"

Step 5: Summarize

Ms. Garcia reviews the main points: the multiplicative relationship between measures in a ratio can be a non-integer value (for example, 1.5) and this relationship is constant for all equivalent ratios (e.g., 3:2, 6:4, 30:20, and so on). Even though these points were brought up in the discussion, she revisits them.

To push students to make their thinking explicit, she asks, "How can there be one and one-half times as many white roses if you can't have half a rose?" Several students demonstrate using materials. Through all of this, Ms. Garcia makes sure students do not lose sight of the original question.

Ms. Garcia poses a similar task:

What is another way to compare the numbers of white and red roses?

Looking Ahead

Now that you have an understanding of what makes a good question (Chapter 1), methods for creating good questions (Chapter 2), and the basics for using good questions in your classroom (Chapter 3), we invite you to explore the second part of this resource, which is filled with our favorite good questions. We hope that you too will find them useful as you incorporate more questioning techniques into your classroom.

PART II

Good Questions to Use in Math Lessons

CHAPTER 4	Good Questions for Number Relationships	23
CHAPTER 5	Good Questions for Multiplication and Proportional Reasoning	53
CHAPTER 6	Good Questions for Fractions, Decimals, and Percentages	79
CHAPTER 7	Good Questions for Geometry	133
CHAPTER 8	Good Questions for Algebraic Thinking	157
CHAPTER 9	Good Questions for Data Analysis and Probability	199
CHAPTER 10	Good Questions for Measurement	231

In Part II, we offer examples of good questions for you to select from and use in your classroom. Each question is accompanied by notes to support your teaching.

The Organization of Questions

The questions are categorized by mathematical topic, each topic organized into two grade spans: grades 5–6 and grades 7–8.

Many of the questions in these spans can be adapted to meet the needs of the students in your classroom by making them easier or more difficult. You may wish to explore questions in both grade spans as you decide on appropriate questions for your particular class. For example, if you teach sixth grade and your students have a thorough understanding of multiplication and proportional reasoning, you may want to explore questions for grades 7–8 within the multiplication and proportional reasoning chapter.

In general, the questions in each span are neither hierarchical nor sequential. Each can be posed individually. Each span can be viewed as an à la carte menu of question choices to help students deepen their understanding of the mathematics they are studying.

The Investigations

As you are reading through the good questions that follow, you will find some instances where they have been written as investigations rather than questions. This has been done where we felt they were better written as investigations. Use them in exactly the same way as the questions.

The List of Experiences

At the beginning of each topic for each grade span is a list of experiences that students should encounter for the particular topic. Not all students will be ready for these experiences at the same time. It is quite possible that some students in grades 7–8 might be working on some of the experiences listed for grades 5–6. The list should not be treated as a progression of experiences but rather as a range of possible experiences.

The List of Materials

A list of materials that you might need is also provided at the beginning of each topic for each span. You will not need all of these materials unless you complete every question listed for the topic in that span. Check that you have suitable materials before you present a question to your class. It is important that students have a variety of concrete materials to select from when they are working on mathematical tasks.

The Teacher Notes

Following most questions there are teacher notes. Some identify important teaching points for the particular question while others describe in more depth the mathematics being addressed or misconceptions that may present themselves. At other times they will be useful in helping you assess students so you can plan to overcome any difficulties. It is a good idea to make notes as you observe students working to use in future planning.

CHAPTER 4

GOOD QUESTIONS FOR NUMBER RELATIONSHIPS

GRADES 5–6	**24**
Factors and Multiples	*24*
Even and Odd	*30*
Polygonal Numbers	*35*
Integers	*39*
GRADES 7–8	**42**
Number Relationships	*42*

When we ask students questions about relationships, properties, and procedures associated with number concepts, we help our students make important mathematical connections between numbers and their representations.

23

OVERVIEW

Factors and Multiples

(Grades 5–6)

The vocabulary of number theory is relatively new to fifth and sixth graders. We need to listen very carefully to the mathematical talk of our students to support their correct use of the terminology. Although many fifth and sixth graders instinctively understand the terms *factor* and *multiple*, it becomes increasingly necessary to offer a variety of experiences in which students can use and apply newly defined mathematical words and classifications.

Experiences at This Level Will Help Students To

- link dimensions of array models with factors and products
- identify relationships among factors, multiples, divisors, and products
- develop strategies to solve problems involving factors and multiples

Reproducibles are available in a downloadable, printable format. See page xx for directions about how to access them.

Materials

- color tiles
- Graph Paper (Reproducible A)
- Dot Paper (Reproducible B)

Good Questions and Teacher Notes (pages 25–29)

24   GOOD QUESTIONS FOR MATH TEACHING

FACTORS AND MULTIPLES (GRADES 5–6)

 1. Study the arrays of these numbers: 12, 24, 36, and 48. What are the properties that could help you classify these numbers into one group? If you added another number to this group, what could it be?

Possible student answers could be:

> They are all divisible by 2. (How do you know?)
> They are all divisible by 12. (Can you show me?)
> They are all divisible by 2 and 3. (Can we make a conjecture about the divisibility rules of 6?)
> They are all divisible by 2 and 4. (Are all numbers divisible by 2 also divisible by 4? Is the reverse true? That is, are all numbers divisible by 4 also divisible by 2?)

Carefully crafted questions that probe the depth of students' understanding, which may be initially fragile, can make for rich classroom discussion. If students are encouraged to support their positions and give mathematical proof as they talk, their understanding will deepen.

 2. Here is a set of numbers: {2, 3, 5, 7, 11, 13, 17}. What do these numbers have in common? How are they alike?

They each have two factor pairs, two arrays, and two factors. They are prime.

Visual representations of numbers and concepts continue to be important for students of this age. This activity gives students the opportunity to create a visual representation for a prime number.

GOOD QUESTIONS FOR MATH TEACHING

GOOD QUESTIONS AND TEACHER NOTES

 3. What do you notice about the array for 1? How is it different from other numbers and their arrays? Support your conjecture with what you already know about prime and composite numbers.

> There is a single array, and it is only 1 by 1. It is neither prime nor composite because it does not fit the classification generalization for either prime or composite numbers.

 4. What other classifications can you use to group numbers? Use arrays and writing to support your groupings. Create sets of numbers and ask others to identify your grouping rule or principle.

> Students may group numbers by divisibility, multiples, exponential progressions (even if they do not realize that that is what they are doing!), odd/even, and so on.

 5. What is the smallest number that has 3 and 4 as factors?

> Questions 5 and 6 have to do with common multiples, but they use factors to identify the product. This can be difficult for some students. It can even be difficult for some adults! If 3 and 4 have no common factors between them other than 1, then the smallest multiple common to both is their product.

FACTORS AND MULTIPLES (GRADES 5–6)

6. What is the smallest number that has 4 and 6 as factors?

> Four and 6 share common factors, so we can assume the common multiple is less than the product of this pair of numbers. Rather than presenting students with a recipe, pose even more questions that will allow them to begin to formulate their own generalizations: Find pairs of numbers for which the common multiple is equal to the product of the pair. Find pairs of numbers for which the common multiple is less than the product of the pair. What do you notice about these two sets of pairs? Which pairs have common factors? Which do not?

7. For a given pair of numbers, how can you tell whether the least common multiple will be less than or equal to their product?

> Questions 5 and 6 lead up to this particular question. Identifying common factors of a pair of numbers can help us determine how to find the least common multiple of that same pair of numbers. Writing about this generalization can reveal students' understandings as well as their misconceptions.

GOOD QUESTIONS FOR MATH TEACHING   27

GOOD QUESTIONS AND TEACHER NOTES

8. Sebastian was gathering baseball equipment for his teammates. He grabbed 81 baseballs and 27 bats. He wants to make sure each teammate receives an equal number of pieces of equipment with no leftovers.

   a. What is the largest number of players Sebastian can have on his baseball team?

   b. How many baseballs and how many bats will each player receive?

> Discerning whether a story problem requires the manipulation of common factors or common multiples is a difficult task for any fifth or sixth grader! In this particular problem, the number of items is fixed—there can be no more or less than 81 baseballs and no more or less than 27 bats. Problems with *fixed totals* requires the use of *greatest common factors*. In this particular problem, Sebastian has 27 players on his team—each player receives 3 baseballs and 1 bat.

9. Stephen and Alexander are in a brownie eating competition. Stephen can finish a brownie every 11 seconds. Alexander can finish a brownie every 12 seconds. They start at the exact same second and continue this pace for the entire competition.

   a. After how many seconds will they start eating a brownie at the same time again?

   b. How many brownies will they have eaten at this point?

> In contrast to the preceding problem, the totals will change to adhere to the constraints of the problem. To solve this problem, finding the *least common multiple* is necessary. Since 11 and 12 are relatively prime and only share one as a common factor, the two numbers are multiplied to identify the least common multiple. Not only is the least common multiple needed, but the number of multiples of each quantity also needs to be identified, which represents how many brownies each boy has eaten.

FACTORS AND MULTIPLES (GRADES 5–6)

10. The weather is reported every 18 minutes on WFAC and every 12 minutes on WTOR. Both stations broadcast the weather at 1:30. When is the next time the stations will broadcast the weather at the same time?

> Common multiple problems are more engaging and challenging when a context is given and when they require an additional step. In this problem, students are not only finding common multiples, but are required to convert minutes into hours as they determine the cycle of time when both stations will broadcast the weather at the same time.

11. How do you know when you have found all of the possible factors for a given number? What is the greatest factor possible for any whole number? Why does this make sense?

> These questions will help students develop efficient strategies for finding factors.

12. Do you think that it makes sense to split a day into twenty-four hours? Would another number have been a better choice? Why or why not?

> Linking mathematical questions to real-life problem solving helps students validate their learning.

GOOD QUESTIONS FOR MATH TEACHING

OVERVIEW

EVEN AND ODD (GRADES 5–6)

EXPERIENCES AT THIS LEVEL WILL HELP STUDENTS TO

- identify characteristics of various number classifications such as even and odd

Reproducibles are available in a downloadable, printable format. See page xx for directions about how to access them.

MATERIALS

- color tiles
- Graph Paper (Reproducible A)
- rules for *Fair Game 2* (Reproducible 1)
- Dot Paper (Reproducible B)

GOOD QUESTIONS AND TEACHER NOTES (PAGES 31–34)

30   GOOD QUESTIONS FOR MATH TEACHING

EVEN AND ODD (GRADES 5–6)

1. What makes 12 an even or odd number? Use an array to support your position.

A discussion of divisibility can begin with this activity. The idea that an array of an even number can be equally divided into two parts can move students beyond the premise that an even number is a "double" and toward the idea that every even number is divisible by 2.

Do not allow students to dismiss questions pertaining to odd and even numbers as too simple. It becomes increasingly important, as well as interesting, to revisit big ideas to assess further understanding and increased conceptual application.

2. Is the sum of two odd numbers odd or even? Is the sum of two even numbers odd or even? What about the sum of an odd and an even number? Justify your thinking using words, symbols, drawings, or color tiles.

Arrays can again be helpful as students work to articulate what constitutes evenness or oddness. The ability to evenly pair up counters (e.g., color tiles) in an array designates an even number whereas leftover counters designate an odd number. Students may also identify the odd-even sequence of counting numbers, which can also determine evenness or oddness. Introducing students to a matrix as an aid to charting outcomes is also of great help.

+	Even	Odd
Even	e	o
Odd	o	e

GOOD QUESTIONS FOR MATH TEACHING

GOOD QUESTIONS AND TEACHER NOTES

 3. Is the product of two odd numbers odd or even? Is the product of two even numbers odd or even? What about the product of an odd and an even number? Justify your thinking using words, symbols, drawings, or color tiles.

> Comparing the outcomes between the addition and multiplication of even and odd numbers can quickly lead to mathematically rich discussions. Issues of probability can generate more thought-provoking questions. For example, you could use this line of questioning with your students: If you were given a point each time you rolled an even sum with two dice and your partner received the same when rolling an odd sum, who would have the better chance of winning? If you were given a point each time you rolled an even product with two dice and your partner received the same when rolling an odd product, who would have a better chance of winning? A matrix is again helpful to chart outcomes.
>
> | × | Even | Odd |
> |------|------|-----|
> | Even | e | e |
> | Odd | e | o |

EVEN AND ODD (GRADES 5–6)

4. Choose a partner and play a game of *Fair Game 2* (Burns 2000). Using what you know about the sums and products of odd and even numbers, answer the following questions: Explain your reasoning for both the addition and the multiplication version. Is either game fair? Which player would you rather be? How could you make the game more fair?

(See Reproducible 1, Fair Game 2.)

Charting the data from these games is important. Students can make conjectures as to the fairness of each game by analyzing their data. They may also realize that the matrices used in answering Questions 2 and 3 can also be helpful in supporting their "fair" or "not fair" positions.

Number Model	Player A Points	Player B Points
5 + 1 = 6	1	0
6 + 1 = 7	0	1
6 + 1 = 7	0	1
3 + 4 = 7	0	1

5. Is 0 an even or an odd number?

The odd-even-odd-even pattern of counting numbers or the odd-even-odd-even distribution of numbers on a number line is helpful in constructing a meaningful answer to this question. Too often, even older elementary-age students consider 0 to be a non-number. Answering this question will cause some shift in thinking about the value of 0 and what it "does" to and for numbers like 20, 200, 2,000, and so on.

GOOD QUESTIONS FOR MATH TEACHING   33

GOOD QUESTIONS AND TEACHER NOTES

6. Make a case for why each number could not belong. Use words such as *factor, multiple, odd, even, prime,* and *composite* to support your position.

24,   12,   2,   11

> Asking students to identify more than one numeric relationship within a given set of numbers will help them develop the flexibility of reasoning often required by mathematical investigations.

7. I am thinking of four odd numbers.

They are divisible by 5.

The sums of the digits of each number create a consecutive number sequence.

My first number is a square number.

What are my four numbers?

> Asking students to generate multiple sets of numbers that comply with an organizing principle can deepen understanding of those classifications. One answer is the numbers 25, 35, 45, and 55.

OVERVIEW

Polygonal Numbers

(Grades 5–6)

Experiences at This Level Will Help Students To

- identify characteristics of various number classifications such as prime, composite, square, and triangular

Reproducibles are available in a downloadable, printable format. See page xx for directions about how to access them.

Materials

- color tiles
- Graph Paper (Reproducible A)
- Dot Paper (Reproducible B)

Good Questions and Teacher Notes (pages 36–38)

GOOD QUESTIONS FOR MATH TEACHING   35

GOOD QUESTIONS AND TEACHER NOTES

 1. Using dot paper, make a 1-by-1 array, a 2-by-2 array, and a 3-by-3 array. Outline the squares.

(See Reproducible B, Dot Paper.)

•   • •   • • •
         • •   • • •
                    • • •

These are the first three "square" numbers. What would the next square number be? Justify your thinking. List or diagram the square numbers up to one hundred. Why are these numbers called square numbers?

> Students are fascinated by patterns, especially those that work for an entire classification of numbers.

 2. What is the tenth square number? How do you know?

> Using the information from Question 1, we can determine that the sixth square number makes a 6-by-6 array, the seventh a 7-by-7 array, and so on. The tenth square number would make a 10-by-10 array. Introducing the use of exponents as a symbolic representation is helpful and contextually relevant.

POLYGONAL NUMBERS (GRADES 5–6)

 3. Can a square number be a prime number? Why or why not?

> Square numbers cannot be prime by definition. They have an odd number of factors (the least number of factors being three) and are the only classification of numbers that do.
>
> Asking students why this is so can help students uncover properties of square numbers.

 4. Which square numbers are odd? Which are even? Can you describe a pattern demonstrated by consecutive square numbers? Will the seventeenth square number be odd or even? What about the eighteenth?

> Generalizing patterns is a fundamental pre-algebraic skill. Connecting words to physical and symbolic representations is a skill too often ignored for students of this age.

 5. I am thinking of a two-digit number. It is odd. It has exactly three factors. What number(s) might I be thinking of? Think of a final clue so that there is just one final solution.

> Once students begin to investigate different topics related to number theory, it becomes increasingly important to link those topics together so that students can begin to develop a web of understanding. Asking students to generate their own number riddles about square numbers (or any other type of number) can support their understanding as well.

GOOD QUESTIONS FOR MATH TEACHING   37

GOOD QUESTIONS AND TEACHER NOTES

 6. These are the first three "triangular" numbers:

•

• •

• • •

• • • •

Diagram the next three triangular numbers on dot paper. What patterns do you see? Describe or diagram the tenth triangular number. What do you know about triangular numbers?

(See Reproducible B, Dot Paper.)

> It may be necessary for students to represent triangular numbers on dot paper before they can generate their properties and/or patterns in words.
>
> Students may want to pose their own questions about triangular numbers. Is there an odd-even sequence? Are any triangular numbers square numbers as well?

OVERVIEW

INTEGERS (Grades 5–6)

EXPERIENCES AT THIS LEVEL WILL HELP STUDENTS TO

- make sense of the set of integers as the set of whole numbers and their opposites
- find the absolute value of an integer
- locate integers on a number line

Reproducibles are available in a downloadable, printable format. See page xx for directions about how to access them.

MATERIALS

- color tiles
- Graph Paper (Reproducible A)
- Dot Paper (Reproducible B)

GOOD QUESTIONS AND TEACHER NOTES (pages 40–41)

GOOD QUESTIONS FOR MATH TEACHING 39

GOOD QUESTIONS AND TEACHER NOTES

1. Josie is working on a homework assignment from class. She is asked to find the "opposites" of integers such as +12 and -48. Josie wonders, "Does every integer have an opposite? Since zero is an integer, does it have an opposite?" What do you think about Josie's question? How would you answer it?

> Every integer will have an opposite since a number line extends infinitely in both directions. A common misconception is that 0 has no opposite when, in fact, it is actually its own opposite.

2. Ibrahim and Jack were placing numbers on a number line. Ibrahim said, "My number is greater than yours." Jack agreed but added, "My number has a greater absolute value than yours." What could Ibrahim and Jack's numbers be?

> Since absolute value is defined as a number's distance from 0, encourage students to use a number line to answer this question and support their solution(s). Jack's number must be negative but farther from 0 than Ibrahim's.

3. Find values that can replace the question marks to create true statements.

   a. -(?) = ?

   b. |?| > ?

   c. |?| < ?

> In addition to providing specific answers, encourage students to generalize. For example, the first statement will be true for any pair of opposites such that the negative integer in the pair is on the left side of the equal sign (e.g., -(-3) = 3).

INTEGERS (GRADES 5–6)

 4. Find values that can fill in the blanks in the sentences below.

   a. The number _____ is a positive integer and is located _____ units to the right of -7 on the number line.

   b. The number _____ is a negative integer and is located _____ units to the right of -10 on the number line.

   c. The number _____ is a negative integer and is located _____ units to the left of +5 on the number line.

   d. The number _____ is a _____ integer and it is as far from 0 as _____ on the number line.

> This question promotes understanding of integers as both *locations* on a number line and *distances* on a number line.

 5. Write an integer addition number sentence for the number line model that follows.

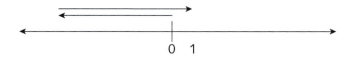

> Encourage students to generalize about their answers. For example, all possible answers have addends of the form "a pair of opposites plus one."

GOOD QUESTIONS FOR MATH TEACHING

OVERVIEW

Number Relationships

(Grades 7–8)

Experiences at This Level Will Help Children To

- relate integers to the set of rational numbers
- operate on integers and positive and negative rational numbers
- read and write very large numbers using exponential and scientific notation
- work with square roots and cube roots
- compare and contrast the sets of rational and irrational numbers
- use rational approximations to compare irrational numbers and locate them on a number line

Materials

- calculators
- rulers

Good Questions and Teacher Notes (pages 43–51)

NUMBER RELATIONSHIPS (GRADES 7–8)

1. Explain how each number below is different from all of the others.

$$81 \quad -\sqrt{81} \quad \frac{2}{3} \quad \sqrt{3}$$

This question offers a great opportunity to explore relationships between integers, rational numbers, and irrational numbers. For example, $\frac{2}{3}$ is the only rational number in the list that is equivalent to a repeating decimal.

2. What number might represent point A on the following number line?

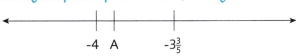

If students only provide answers that are rational numbers, encourage them to find possible values that are irrational numbers.

3. Find a number that satisfies each of the descriptions that follow.

   a. A number that is a little less than 4 units to the left of 0 on a number line

   b. A number that is a little more than 5 units to the left of +1 on a number line

   c. A number that is a little less than 3 units to the right of -10 on a number line.

You can adapt this question by asking students to find rational or irrational numbers (e.g., an irrational number that is a little less than 4 units to the left of 0 on a number line).

GOOD QUESTIONS FOR MATH TEACHING   43

GOOD QUESTIONS AND TEACHER NOTES

4. For homework, Kim Lee was adding two rational numbers. He looked at a computation and said, "I know the sign of the sum will be negative." Based on Kim Lee's statement, what do you know about the computation?

> This question aims to help students generalize about the relationship between the sign of the sum and the signs of the addends. Students may need to make a list of addition problems whose sums are negative and look for commonalities among them in order to answer this question.

5. Nastia used the following number line to model the addition of two rational numbers. What two rational numbers might she have been adding?

> This question promotes understanding of an addend in terms of distance. One possible answer is 3 + -4.3. In this example, the second addend represents a distance of 4.3 units; the sum is -1.3 because that is the number that is located 4.3 units to the left of +3 on a number line.

44   GOOD QUESTIONS FOR MATH TEACHING

NUMBER RELATIONSHIPS (GRADES 7–8)

 6. Zach looked at an integer subtraction computation and said, "You can find the difference between these two integers by doubling the first integer." What might the computation have been?

> Make a list of students' answers and ask them what they notice. Each computation will be a pair of integer opposites. Once students discover this, link this idea to multiplying the first integer by two. For example, -7 – 7 = -14 can also be written as -7 × 2 = -14.

 7. Replace *a*, *b*, *c*, and *d* with a number to create a true inequality.

   a. $3.73 - a < 0$

   b. $b + 214.3 < 0$

   c. $c - (-4\frac{1}{2}) < 0$

   d. $d + (-5\frac{3}{4}) < 0$

> Once students find several answers, discuss generalizations about the conditions on each variable.

 8. Mannie multiplied three integers on his calculator and got a product of -48. What might the integers have been?

> Post students' answers to this question and ask them what generalizations they notice among them. Doing so will help students understand the relationships between the signs of factors and corresponding products.

GOOD QUESTIONS FOR MATH TEACHING

GOOD QUESTIONS AND TEACHER NOTES

 9. Find values for *a* and *b* such that $\frac{a}{b}$ = -8 where neither *a* nor *b* is an integer.

> This question encourages students to think deeply about the relationship between rational numbers (i.e., numbers that can be written as a ratio of two integers) and integers (whole numbers and their opposites). One possible answer is $-\frac{\frac{8}{3}}{\frac{1}{3}}$ = -8

 10. Nan's Donut Shop has been in business for one month. Each week, Nan looks at her income and expenses to determine her profit (income − expenses = profit). Nan has determined that her average weekly profit is -$40. What might have been Nan's income and expenses each week?

> If students are unfamiliar with using money to learn about integers, you may need to discuss what -$40 means before asking students to answer this question.

NUMBER RELATIONSHIPS (GRADES 7–8)

 11. Katya earns $5 a day in allowance and spends $3 a day on lunch and other necessities. What number sentence could Katya use to determine how much money she has after any number of days?

> Student-generated number sentences might include the following:
>
> $(5 \times n) - (3 \times n) = t$
> $5n - (3n) = t$
> $2n = t$
>
> where n = number of days; t = total amount of money
>
> Ask students to identify what is the same and what is different among their answers. Comparing and contrasting number sentences will help students identify relationships among them.

 12. Niles kept track of the temperature outside his home from noon until midnight. Upon looking back at the data, he noticed that the rule $50 + (-0.5)h = t$ (where h equals the number of hours after noon and t equals the temperature) could be used to approximate the temperature at any given time. How did the temperature change over the course of this day?

> Too often students can plug values into expressions that use variables without understanding the expressions. It is just as important to spend time discussing the meaning of expressions as it is to evaluate them.

GOOD QUESTIONS FOR MATH TEACHING   47

13. The population of the United States is estimated to be 3.3×10^8. What might be the actual population?

Exploring scientific notation using real-world data makes the topic relevant to students in the middle grades. For homework, have students investigate populations of other countries and represent the data using scientific notation.

14. A popular new album has earned 12.3 million dollars in sales. What might be the actual sales?

Discussing students' answers to this question offers an opportunity to review elementary place-value concepts in the middle grades.

15. Rich used his calculator to estimate how many times his heart has beaten since birth. After he did a series of calculations to determine this number, "4.79E8" appeared on the calculator's screen. How might Rich have interpreted this number?

Students need to learn how to use calculators, like any other tool, to solve problems. For example, students often need to figure out how to interpret the number that appears on the screen. While the output styles vary, calculators often use the notation shown here to express numbers that are too large to fit on the screen. Scientific notation can be used to interpret these numbers. For example, 4.79E8 means that the number is close to 4.79×10^8, or 479,000,000.

NUMBER RELATIONSHIPS (GRADES 7–8)

16. Randy needed to estimate the size of a square root. He looked at the square root and said, "Well, I know it is between ten and eleven." What do you think the square root was?

> Estimating the size of square roots is an important part of developing number sense in the middle grades.

17. Place one square root, one cube root, one integer, and one fraction on the number line. How did you decide where to place your numbers?

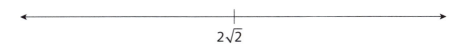
$2\sqrt{2}$

> If students struggle to answer this question, ask them to place 0 on the number line and think about doubling or halving the distance from 0 to $2\sqrt{2}$. This question can be modified by changing the requirements or the given square root.

18. Kaelen used the Pythagorean theorem to measure the hypotenuse of a right triangle. She reported that the hypotenuse was between eight and nine units. What might have been the measurements of the legs of the triangle?

> While this question may be better classified as a measurement question, it offers students a meaningful application of square roots. One way to answer this question is to think of 8 as $\sqrt{64}$ and 9 as $\sqrt{81}$. Then, find two numbers whose squares have a sum that is greater than 64 but less than 81.

GOOD QUESTIONS FOR MATH TEACHING   49

GOOD QUESTIONS AND TEACHER NOTES

19. In math class, Brianna used the Pythagorean theorem to find the measurement of the hypotenuse of a right triangle whose legs measured two inches and three inches. Once she found the measurement, $\sqrt{13}$, her teacher said, "Use your ruler to check your answers." But Brianna said, "How can I use my ruler when it does not show square roots?" What do you think Brianna's teacher had in mind? How could Brianna have used a ruler to check her answers?

> Using a ruler to explore square roots will help students approximate the size of square roots using what they know about whole numbers and fractions.

20. Mateo used the following steps to express the perimeter of an isosceles right triangle whose side lengths measured $\sqrt{8}$, $\sqrt{8}$, and 4 units:

$\sqrt{8} + \sqrt{8} = \sqrt{16} = 4$

$4 + 4 = 8$

Perimeter = 8 units

What do you think of Mateo's method?

> Students often think that $\sqrt{a} + \sqrt{b} = \sqrt{a+b}$. This is a common misconception that can be addressed by estimating the size of the square roots being added. For example, $\sqrt{8}$ is greater than 2 since $\sqrt{4} = 2$. The sum of $\sqrt{8} + \sqrt{8}$ would, therefore, be greater than 4, not equal to 4.

50 GOOD QUESTIONS FOR MATH TEACHING

NUMBER RELATIONSHIPS (GRADES 7–8)

21. The volume of Cube B is greater than the volume of Cube A and close to but less than the volume of Cube C. What might be the measure of its side?

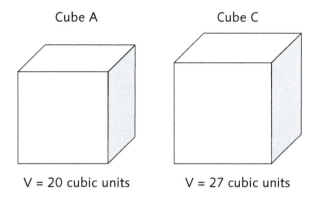

Cube A
V = 20 cubic units

Cube C
V = 27 cubic units

Students can express their answers in terms of cube roots (e.g., $\sqrt[3]{26}$ units) or as approximations (e.g., 2.84 units).

GOOD QUESTIONS FOR MATH TEACHING

CHAPTER 5

Good Questions for Multiplication and Proportional reasoning

GRADES 5–6	54
Multiplication and Proportional Reasoning	*54*
GRADES 7–8	**70**
Multiplication and Proportional Reasoning	*70*

The study of multiplication, division, and proportional reasoning can promote procedural competency and conceptual understanding. Facility with multiplicative and proportional reasoning builds a foundation for the study of formal algebra later on (Lobato and Ellis 2010). Asking questions that require students to make sense of multiplication and division and explore proportional relationships is an effective way to prepare them for this work.

OVERVIEW

Multiplication and Proportional Reasoning

(Grades 5–6)

Although procedural competency is an important goal in the teaching of multiplication and division, the questions in this section are designed to promote and establish further conceptual understanding and knowledge of these operations.

Experiences at This Level Will Help Students To

- understand the language of multiplication and division situations
- refine methods of multiplication and division
- decompose factors to make sense of multiplicative properties and procedures
- interpret two types of division situations: partitive and quotative
- interpret remainders within the context of a story problem
- apply rules of divisibility
- use language associated with ratios
- represent proportional relationships using words, pictures, tables, and numbers
- set up and solve proportions

Reproducibles are available in a downloadable, printable format. See page xx for directions about how to access them.

Materials

- calculators
- colored pencils
- Graph Paper (Reproducible A)

Good Questions and Teacher Notes (pages 55–69)

54 GOOD QUESTIONS FOR MATH TEACHING

MULTIPLICATION AND PROPORTIONAL REASONING (GRADES 5–6)

1. ? × ? = 612

What might the missing numbers be? Can you find more than one solution? Explain. Use one of the number models you found to create a story problem. Include the missing factors in your story problem.

Finding missing factors can give students valuable calculating and estimating experiences.

2. How could this array model help you solve 5 × 8? Or 15 × 4? Explain your thinking in number models as you compare factors and products.

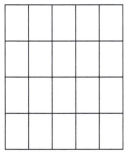

Identifying the manipulation of factors or products will allow students the ability to use what they know to figure out what they do not know as well as how to work within an equation to solve for unknowns.

Moving to naked number sequences can further extend these flexible thinking opportunities for students. A whole-class activity such as *Silent Multiplication* as referenced in *Teaching Arithmetic: Lessons for Extending Multiplication* (Wickett and Burns 2001) can offer additional opportunities to practice and extend the proportional manipulation of factors or products.

GOOD QUESTIONS FOR MATH TEACHING

GOOD QUESTIONS AND TEACHER NOTES

3. Create a story problem that involves multiplying the factors 36 and 17. Give a written explanation of how you could solve the problem.

> Written explanations of solutions can help identify understandings and misconceptions. Story problems written by students of this age should demonstrate multiplicative relationships rather than additive (repeated addition) ones.

4. Calculate the solutions to these multiplication problems. How can you explain the pattern you can use to find the products when multiplying by zeros?

$200 \times 300 =$ _____ $500 \times 500 =$ _____
$60 \times 80 =$ _____ $4 \times 900 =$ _____
$100 \times 800 =$ _____ $20 \times 80 =$ _____

How could you adjust your explanation to articulate the pattern you notice when completing these calculations?

$30 \times 18 =$ _____ $343 \times 90 =$ _____
$53 \times 80 =$ _____ $24 \times 400 =$ _____
$118 \times 40 =$ _____ $123 \times 300 =$ _____

> As students work to make sense of the multiplication process, it becomes increasingly important for their shortcuts to be grounded in understanding. Articulating patterns and justifying shortcuts will help students better understand why and how multiplication works.

MULTIPLICATION AND PROPORTIONAL REASONING (GRADES 5–6)

> Questions 5, 6, and 7 follow a possible progression of teaching and thinking in order to help students make sense of multidigit multiplication. It can be helpful for students to discover important multiplicative principles as they work to solve problems. The ability to identify and generalize patterns will support their learning and help them articulate why multiplication works as it does. Each question could take a period—or a week! Valuable multiplication practice will occur as students work to explain and support their solutions, particularly when asked, "Will this work for all groups of numbers?" You may need to make instructional decisions about the amount of time you want to spend on these questions.

5. **How could you break apart 235 to make 235 × 7 a simpler problem? Would that work for any number? Explain and support your reasoning with other examples.**

> 235 × 7 = (200 × 7) + (30 × 7) + (5 × 7)
>
> Students can easily lose sight of the necessity of preserving place value when multiplying. Activities that require students to decompose numbers remind them of the magnitude of each single digit within a larger number.

GOOD QUESTIONS AND TEACHER NOTES

6. Construct a 14-by-23 array on a piece of graph paper. Using colored pencils, partition the array to model the following equation:

14 × 23 = (10 × 20) + (10 × 3) + (4 × 20) + (4 × 3).

Are there other ways to partition this array? Why or why not? If so, use number models to identify different ways to partition this array.

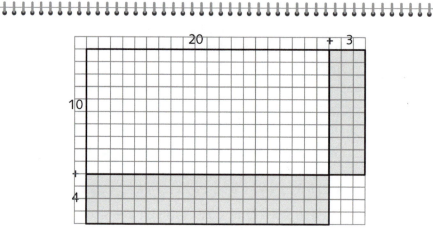

A model of a 14-by-23 array partitioned into the four sections.

Array models allow students to visually decompose factors to make for friendlier, perhaps more manageable, multiplications. There will be those students who will find this model of multiplication and this type of activity powerful. The ability to decompose factors becomes visible and meaningful.

Activities such as this can lead students to important discoveries and understandings about the distributive property. Asking students to apply their proofs to other multiplication problems will allow them to make important generalizations. Asking a follow-up question such as, "Will this work with all two-digit numbers?" will give students additional opportunities to apply the distributive property.

MULTIPLICATION AND PROPORTIONAL REASONING (GRADES 5–6)

 7. How could you break apart each factor to make 58 × 46 an easier problem? What problem could you start with? How could you make sure you had completed all the multiplications required by this problem? Will this work for every two-digit multiplication problem?

> An understanding of number sense, place value, and the application of the distributive property is necessary in the construction of a partial-products algorithm. There are several procedures that could be employed, such as 58 × 46 = (50 + 8) × (40 + 6).
>
> There will be four multiplications:
>
> 50 × 40
> 50 × 6
> 8 × 40
> 8 × 6
>
> Changing the factors to 60 × 46 is also a possibility. Some interesting and valuable understandings, as well as misconceptions, about how to handle those two extra 46s can come about using this strategy. Since we have added two extra 46s, now what do we do with them to get back to our original problem?
>
> The application of and generalizations made about the distributive property are more important than the recitation of the property itself at the fifth- and sixth-grade levels.

GOOD QUESTIONS FOR MATH TEACHING

GOOD QUESTIONS AND TEACHER NOTES

8. Study the progression of factors and products. How does each equation build on the equation that precedes it?

6 × 7 = 42	5 × 9 = 45
60 × 7 = 420	5 × 90 = 450
60 × 14 = 840	5 × 45 = 225
30 × 14 = 420	50 × 45 = 2,250
15 × 14 = 210	25 × 45 = 1,125

The pre-algebraic concept of balance, or equivalence, can begin to develop from these sequences and questions. If a factor is doubled, then so too is the product. If a product is halved, then so is one of the factors. The visual image of keeping both sides of an equation balanced is very helpful to fifth and sixth graders.

Creating these sequences is extremely helpful for both teachers and students. It gives all of us the opportunity to mentally play with factors and products.

9. Using the numbers 1, 2, 3, and 4:

Create the *largest* product by filling in the blanks:

__ __ × __ __   __ __ __ × __

Create the *smallest* product by filling in the blanks:

__ __ × __ __   __ __ __ × __

How does the order of the digits affect the product?

Applying discovered generalizations can strengthen multiplicative thinking, estimating, and problem solving. Problems such as these often create valuable calculating practice. Additional questions using the numbers 5, 6, 7, and 8 could also be constructed to support generalizations.

MULTIPLICATION AND PROPORTIONAL REASONING (GRADES 5–6)

10. Which of the following problems has the largest product? Try to figure it out by solving as few problems as possible. How did you choose which problems to do or not do?

42 × 17	24 × 12	52 × 11
40 × 20	50 × 24	43 × 16
36 × 36	12 × 14	42 × 42

> Although this looks like a question about calculation, it is perhaps more about place value, estimation, and the effects of multiplication. Listening to students' strategies as they explain which problems they chose to do or not to do gives teachers valuable insights as to how students think about numbers and what happens to their magnitude when they are multiplied.

11. Write a story about what life might be like if suddenly something became "ten times more." For example, what would life be like if your math teacher gave you ten times more math homework a night? Or what would life be like if mosquitoes were ten times as big? Use your imagination but be specific. Give counts or measurements to support your story.

> At this age, students are beginning to encounter multiplicative comparison situations but have some difficulty knowing what to do with them! Writing a story can create a visual image as well as reinforce the magnitude of multiplication by ten.
>
> Follow-up division stories could be written within the context of ten times less. What would life be like if math class were ten times shorter? What would life be like if you suddenly became ten times smaller?

GOOD QUESTIONS FOR MATH TEACHING

GOOD QUESTIONS AND TEACHER NOTES

12. Dee Vide wanted to solve $\frac{568}{8}$ and $\frac{2{,}306}{6}$ in this way:

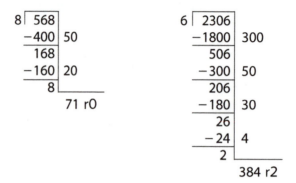

How does this method of division work? Why does it make sense? What could you name this procedure? Could you think of other ways to solve these problems?

> This partial-products division algorithm has begun to be a procedure of choice for many young mathematicians because the dividend remains a complete number, even after the subtractions. Students are often more quickly able to make sense of this procedure and of the division involved than of the standard algorithm.

13. Mrs. Candrive's class has been collecting aluminum cans to recycle. Her first-period class has collected approximately 500 cans. There are twenty-four students in her class. How many cans might each student have collected if each student collected an equal amount? Give a written explanation to justify your solution.

> This division situation can be classified as *partitive*. We know how many groups into which to divide the cans (twenty-four groups). What we do not know is how many objects (cans) are in each group.

62   GOOD QUESTIONS FOR MATH TEACHING

MULTIPLICATION AND PROPORTIONAL REASONING (GRADES 5–6)

14. Mrs. Candrive's class continues to collect aluminum cans to recycle. Each student in her third-period class has collected the same amount of cans. The third-period class has collected almost 300 cans total. How many students might be in the third-period class? Give a written explanation to justify your solution.

> This division situation can be classified as *quotative*. In quotative division situations, the number of objects (cans) in each group is known, but the number of groups (number of students) is not.
>
> It is important to include division situations that require both partitive and quotative manipulation in instruction. If students are presented with just one division situation, they will find it difficult to make sense of the other.

15. Solve this sequence of story problems:

    - Twenty-five fifth graders are going to the Red Sox game. Four fifth graders can be seated in one car. How many cars will be needed to get the fifth graders to Fenway Park?
    - Howard, a baseball fanatic, has $25 in his pocket. Red Sox pennants cost $4 each. How many pennants can Howard buy?
    - Remember Howard? He still has $25 in his pocket. And he still wants to buy pennants that cost $4 each. How much money will he have left to put toward a Fenway Frank (hot dog) if he buys six pennants?
    - Howard decided not to buy the pennants. Who needs six pennants anyway? And he still has that $25. Howard realizes he can buy four baseballs instead. How much does each baseball cost?

    How is each story problem the same? How are they different? In what way does the remainder affect the solution of each problem?

GOOD QUESTIONS FOR MATH TEACHING

GOOD QUESTIONS AND TEACHER NOTES

Remainders happen! Context gives students the opportunity to determine what should be done with a remainder. Should it

- cause the quotient to be rounded up to the next whole number (as in the first solution)?
- be ignored (as in the second solution)?
- be the solution to the problem (as in the third solution)?
- be written as a fraction or a decimal (as in the fourth solution)?

Students will quickly realize that the number model for each story problem is the same. What they may not realize right away is how the remainder determines the solution. The importance of carefully reading story problems and understanding what is being asked is often overlooked by students and teachers alike. In this particular context, the reading becomes as important as the arithmetic.

It is always possible to change the context to fit a particular class or geographic area. If the Red Sox context does not work for you or your students, try changing the sports team or city to fit your needs.

Students may enjoy creating their own story problem sequences such as the one in this question. Choosing simple-division number models can set the stage for wonderfully creative story problems. Having students share and categorize problems as to how the remainder is used can help them strengthen important understandings about solutions derived from division.

MULTIPLICATION AND PROPORTIONAL REASONING (GRADES 5–6)

 16. Write a story problem that matches this expression: $\frac{127}{5}$. Will there be a remainder? How do you know?

> Writing story problems that match division expressions can be difficult for fifth and sixth graders. Their understanding of how to match the procedure to a context can be fragile. If a student presents a "wrong" context, it is helpful to rework the problem as a class in order to make it fit the expression. Class conversations can help to identify misconceptions and move students toward increased understanding of the language nuances of division. Accessibility of and facility with divisibility rules will allow students to quickly realize that this problem will have a remainder without calculation because 127 is not divisible by 5.

 17. Create a story problem and matching number model whose solution has a remainder of 18. How does the remainder affect the solution of your story problem? What strategy did you use to create the number model? How would you adjust your number model to obtain a remainder of 17? A remainder of 19?

> Problems with missing divisors and dividends can offer additional calculating and estimation practice. Students may try several division problems (or multiplication problems) and develop estimation strategies in order to adhere to the constraints of the problem.

GOOD QUESTIONS FOR MATH TEACHING

GOOD QUESTIONS AND TEACHER NOTES

 18. Are the answers below correct? If you think an answer is incorrect, tell whether the given answer is too large or too small. *Then* calculate to see if you were correct.

$$\frac{8,638}{7} = 123.4 \qquad \frac{5,076}{9} = 564$$

$$\frac{696}{8} = 5,568 \qquad \frac{6,785}{5} = 1,357$$

$$\frac{2,428}{4} = 67 \qquad \frac{2,961}{6} = 49.35$$

> Assessing the reasonableness of an answer can at times be more helpful than finding the solution. Sharing strategies can help students validate their thinking, number sense, and understanding of division.

 19. What three-digit number can be divisible by 2, 5, and 10? Explain your thinking.

> Questions such as this relate to students' ability to apply and manipulate divisibility rules. A question that has an unlimited number of solutions quickly engages students. Not only will students find numbers that work, but they will also discover numbers that will not work and why. Encourage students to question their answers!
>
> The solution needs to be even (divisible by 2), and it must end with a zero (divisible by 10, which also means it is divisible by 5). Possible solutions include 180 and 770.

GOOD QUESTIONS FOR MATH TEACHING

MULTIPLICATION AND PROPORTIONAL REASONING (GRADES 5–6)

 20. What three- (or four- or five- or six- . . .) digit number can be divisible by 2, 3, 5, and 6? Explain your thinking.

Solutions need to be

- even (divisible by 2)
- divisible by 3 (the sum of the digits is divisible by 3)
- divisible by 6 (if the number is divisible by 2 *and* 3, then it is also divisible by 6)
- divisible by 5 (the number ends in 5 or 0)

Possible solutions include 150 and 330.

Post students' answers. Ask students if their numbers meet the given criteria. Do students realize that all of their numbers are also divisible by 30? Why is that so?

 21. What four- (or five- or six- . . .) digit number can be divisible by 2, 6, and 9? Explain your thinking.

Solutions need to be

- even (divisible by 2)
- divisible by 3 (to be divisible by 6, the number needs to be divisible by 2 and 3)
- divisible by 9 (the sum of the digits is divisible by 9; any number divisible by 9 is also divisible by 3)

Possible solutions include 6,372 and 1,206.

GOOD QUESTIONS FOR MATH TEACHING   67

GOOD QUESTIONS AND TEACHER NOTES

 22. Green Giant fertilizer and water are mixed in the ratio of one part fertilizer to two parts water. Complete the following chart:

Fertilizer	100 ml	25 ml	?	1.5 L	?	?
Water	200 ml	?	250 ml	?	4 L	490 ml

If you have 410 milliliters of water in your sprayer and 115 milliliters of Green Giant fertilizer left in the original container, can you make a full-strength solution? If you cannot, will the solution be weaker or stronger than it needs to be? How much more water or fertilizer would you need to make a full-strength solution?

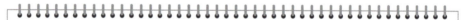

Determining the proportional relationship between a divisor and a dividend can be helpful when students are working to make sense of the division process. Questions that require students to identify proportional relationships between two quantities can help support and develop this reasoning skill. Asking students about the weakness or strength of the solution pushes their understanding of the numerical relationships.

 23. Use the information in Column A to help you complete the other columns.

	A	B	C	D
Sugar	16 oz.	32 oz.	?	14 oz.
Flour	4 oz.	?	7 oz.	?

What is the ratio of sugar to flour?

Decomposing divisors and dividends into smaller, "friendlier" numbers depends on a student's ability to think about numbers and their proportional relationship to each other.

MULTIPLICATION AND PROPORTIONAL REASONING (GRADES 5–6)

24. A 32-gram serving of Cinnamon Life contains 9 grams of sugar. A 55-gram serving of Raisin Nut Bran contains 16 grams of sugar. (Both are $\frac{3}{4}$ cup servings.) Which cereal has less sugar per gram of cereal? How do you know?

> Answering this question could present challenges as well as many different strategies! The problem presented is not the same as in Questions 22 and 23. Students are being asked to compare two different proportions, which extends the thinking required in the previous two questions.
>
> Looking at ratios and playing around with relative equivalence can be helpful for this particular question. The division is not particularly difficult. It is the interpretation of that division that can be powerful.

25. Last year the Salem Sluggers won nine out of every thirteen games. Yu-jin thinks this means that they won nine in a row and then lost four in a row. Do you agree or disagree? Why?

> This question confronts the misconception that the comparison of games won to those played describes the games *consecutively*. To help students with this misconception, ask them to describe a sequence of wins and losses in a twenty-six-game season that results in a nine-to-thirteen ratio. Students will see that varying orders of wins and losses can result in the given ratio.

GOOD QUESTIONS FOR MATH TEACHING   69

OVERVIEW

Multiplication and Proportional Reasoning

(Grades 7–8)

Experiences at This Level Will Help Students To

- Recognize multiplicative and proportional relationships in real-world situations
- Use ratios with rational number measures (e.g., $\frac{1}{2} : \frac{3}{4}$)
- Represent proportional relationships using words, tables, graphs, and equations
- Identify and calculate unit rates
- Set up and solve proportions

Reproducibles are available in a downloadable, printable format. See page xx for directions about how to access them.

Materials

- calculators
- Graph Paper (Reproducible A)
- rulers

Good Questions and Teacher Notes (pages 71–78)

70   GOOD QUESTIONS FOR MATH TEACHING

MULTIPLICATION AND PROPORTIONAL REASONING (GRADES 7–8)

1. A vase holds red and white roses only. There are 1.5 times as many red roses as white roses. How many flowers might be in the vase?

> This question focuses on connecting ratios to multiplicative comparisons. Be sure to spend some time discussing the relationship between the phrase "1.5 times as many" and the ratio 3:2.

2. At hockey practice, Vinod kept track of his number of successful shots on goal and his number of missed shots. At the end of the session he said, "I made two and a half times as many shots as I missed." What fraction of Vinod's attempts might have been goals?

> Vinod is comparing one part of his data set with another. In order to answer the question, students must translate this part-to-part comparison to one that compares a part with the whole. One possible answer is that Vinod made fifteen shots and missed six, so that $\frac{15}{21}$ or $\frac{5}{7}$ of his attempts were goals.

3. Nan and Tim each calculated their walking rates and reported them to each other:

Nan: "I walk a twenty-eight-minute mile."

Tim: "I walk one-half mile every one-quarter hour."

Compare the two students' walking rates.

> One way to compare the two students' walking rates is to find a unit rate for each student. For example, if Nan walks a 28-minute mile, she walks 1 mile every 28 minutes. Since Tim walks $\frac{1}{2}$ mile every $\frac{1}{4}$ hour, he walks 1 mile every 30 minutes. So, Nan walks faster than Tim.

GOOD QUESTIONS FOR MATH TEACHING

GOOD QUESTIONS AND TEACHER NOTES

 4. Sam's Sub Shop offers submarine sandwiches of various lengths. There is a proportional relationship between the length of a sandwich and its price. What might be the price of each sandwich?

Sandwich	Price
Individual Sub (10 inches)	
Footlong Sub (1 foot)	
The Sub for Sharing (18 inches)	
The Crowd Pleaser (4.5 feet)	

One way to answer this question is to choose a price for one sandwich, calculate an associated unit rate (e.g., dollars per inch) and then use this rate to determine the prices of the other sandwiches. Ask students to investigate prices of different sizes of particular foods and drinks at local restaurants to see if the prices are proportional to size.

 5. Approximately 11 percent of the population is left-handed. Use this information to estimate the total number of lefties in this school.

Instead of telling students how many students are in the school, encourage students to use proportional reasoning to estimate the number of students in the school (e.g., number of students in their class times the number of classes in their grade times the number of grades in the school).

MULTIPLICATION AND PROPORTIONAL REASONING (GRADES 7–8)

6. The population density of Omar's town is 212.4 people per square mile. The town is 5 square miles in area. How many people might actually live in each square mile?

> Students sometimes have the misconception that population density represents the actual number of people per square mile as opposed to the average number of people per square mile. Answering this question will help them make this distinction.
>
> Students can investigate the population density of their town, county, or state.

7. Students in one middle school signed up to play basketball, soccer, or volleyball.

   - The number of students who signed up for basketball was about three times greater than the number of students who signed up for soccer.
   - Two out of every five students signed up for basketball.

   How many students might have signed up for each sport?

> Once students find quantities that satisfy the given statements, ask students to use ratios and comparative language to make other conclusions. (Note: The question assumes one sport per student.)

GOOD QUESTIONS FOR MATH TEACHING

GOOD QUESTIONS AND TEACHER NOTES

 8. Claire made a scale drawing of a large banner she plans to create for the school pep rally. The measurements for the length and the width of the banner will actually contain fractions, but she chose a scale so that the drawing had whole-number measurements. What might have been the scale Claire used? Using this scale, what might have been the measurements of Claire's drawing and the measurements of the actual banner?

> One way to engage students in a discussion of this question is to ask a student to reveal their answers to the first two parts of this question and then ask the rest of the class to figure out what that student's answer to the third part must be.

 9. Florida grapefruits are on sale for three for $1.45. One dozen California grapefruits offer a better buy. How much might the California grapefruits cost?

> Comparing and contrasting students' solution methods will help them generalize the proportionality that is present in all methods. Students can write their own "better buy" problems using newspaper circulars and online ads.

 10. A friend of mine walks an 18-minute mile. How many miles per hour must I walk in order to walk faster than her?

> This question helps students make sense of and compare two common unit rates—minutes per mile and miles per hour.

74 GOOD QUESTIONS FOR MATH TEACHING

MULTIPLICATION AND PROPORTIONAL REASONING (GRADES 7–8)

 11. Runner A ran 12 miles in 1 hour and 20 minutes. Runner B ran 18 miles in $2\frac{1}{2}$ hours. Write at least two statements comparing the runners' speeds.

> Extend this question by asking students to find the possible speed for another runner who ran faster than one of the runners here but slower than the other.

 12. The ratio of campers to counselors at Camp Brady is five to two. As enrollment changes, so too must the number of counselors. Create a table, graph, or equation that the camp directors can use to determine the number of counselors, *y*, for any number of campers, *x*.

> Be sure to spend time talking about the relationship between the ratio 5 to 2 and the associated unit rate $\frac{2}{5}$. Since the number of counselors is $\frac{2}{5}$ the number of campers, we can use the equation $y = \frac{2}{5}x$ to model the relationship between number of campers, *x*, and number of counselors, *y*.

 13. Sarintino's restaurant provides two food servers for every nine guests. Zapoteka restaurant seats 135 guests and boasts a better food-server-to-guest ratio. How many food servers might it have?

> Since the ratio 2:9 is equivalent to 30:135, Zapoteka needs more than thirty food servers.

GOOD QUESTIONS FOR MATH TEACHING

GOOD QUESTIONS AND TEACHER NOTES

14. The ratio of cats to dogs in a neighborhood is exactly 2.4 to 1. How many cats and how many dogs might be in this neighborhood?

> In addition to sharing students' answers, discuss ways to interpret and make sense of the ratio 2.4 cats to 1 dog. For example, this ratio conveys that there are almost two and a half times as many cats as dogs.

15. Chip-a-Choo Cookie Company boasts "1,000 chips in every bag!" How could we determine whether this claim is true without counting the chips in every cookie?

> One strategy is to take a sample of cookies, find the average number of chips in that sample, and then multiply the average by the total number of cookies in the bag.

16. Mrs. Kilban drove 30 miles in 1 hour at varying speeds. Describe the different speeds she might have driven at, how long she traveled at them, and how far she got while driving at each speed.

> While miles per hour is a common unit rate, in reality speeds are rarely maintained for a full hour. As a result, students need as much experience scaling down unit rates as they do scaling them up.

MULTIPLICATION AND PROPORTIONAL REASONING (GRADES 7–8)

 17. A proportional relationship between two variables, *x* and *y*, is graphed on a coordinate grid. The graph contains the point (8, 10). Is this enough information to sketch the graph of the relationship between *x* and *y*? Why or why not?

> Yes, this is enough information since the graph must also go through point (0, 0). Be sure to also discuss the relationship between the given ordered pair (8, 10) and the rate of change for the relationship ($\frac{10}{8}$).

 18. A proportional relationship between two variables, *x* and *y*, is represented by a graph that contains the point (-1, $\frac{3}{4}$). What else do you know about this relationship?

> Because the relationship is proportional, we know that the rate of change is *y/x*. So that gives us $\frac{3}{4}$: -1 or -$\frac{3}{4}$ for the rate of change between x and y. This is enough information to represent the relationship between the variables with the equation $y = -\frac{3}{4}x$.

GOOD QUESTIONS FOR MATH TEACHING

GOOD QUESTIONS AND TEACHER NOTES

 19. What values might replace the question marks to make a true proportion?

$$\frac{?}{12} = \frac{7}{?}$$

> This question offers a great opportunity to talk about the invariant multiplicative relationship within a ratio (*a:b*) and the covariant multiplicative relationship across equivalent ratios. For example, if students choose 2 as the missing value in the ratio on the left, since 2 × 6 = 12, the other missing value must be 7 × 6 or 42. Also, because we must multiply each measure in a ratio by the same scale factor to create an equivalent ratio, we know that since 2 × 3.5 = 7, then the other missing value must be 12 × 3.5 or 42.

CHAPTER 6

GOOD QUESTIONS FOR FRACTIONS, DECIMALS, AND PERCENTAGES

GRADES 5–6	81
Fractions	*81*
Decimals	*99*
Percentages	*110*
GRADES 7–8	**115**
Fractions	*115*
Decimals	*121*
Percentages	*126*

As they enter the middle grades, the focus of students' work in mathematics moves beyond whole numbers to the set of rational numbers. A key goal of mathematics instruction in grades 5–8 is to develop a deep understanding of rational number concepts, become proficient in rational number computation and estimation, and learn to think flexibly about relationships among fractions, decimals, and percentages (Barnett-Clarke et al. 2010). Carefully crafted questions can help support our students as they work toward conceptual and procedural understanding of rational numbers.

Much time is spent studying fractions, decimals, and percentages in the fifth and sixth grades. It has become increasingly evident that fractions, decimals, and percentages are too often manipulated by rote by both teachers and students rather than by conceptual and procedural understandings. Many of the following questions concentrate on the construction of meaningful procedures and strategies supported by conceptual understandings. Often students perceive fractions and decimals as two separate units of study. Their equivalence and interchangeability are often overlooked as we rush to teach computational skills. Whenever possible, symbolically represent decimals as fractions

GOOD QUESTIONS FOR FRACTIONS, DECIMALS, AND PERCENTAGES

($0.25 = \frac{25}{100}$). When speaking of decimals, using the language of "tenths" or "hundredths" instead of "point five" or "point twenty-five" can help students make the important connections between decimals and fractions. Weaving percentages into our classroom conversations, activities, and questions can also help students make the necessary connections between fractional, decimal, and percentage notation and representation. Using language such as "per hundred" or "for every hundred" when discussing percentages can be helpful for students as they move from one representation to another.

Some teachers may feel that some of these questions will be too easy for their students. Students can often manipulate fractions, find common denominators, and solve addition and subtraction problems without context with apparent ease. We also find, however, that the rote manipulation of fractions cannot compensate for a lack of understanding of fractional relationships. There will frequently be that handful of students who resist this type of instruction and questioning because they believe that they have mastered the given procedure. Asking students to justify their reasoning and to prove their answers whether with models or symbolic representations becomes increasingly important as we help students construct computational proficiency, efficiency, and understanding. It is equally important to construct questions that will allow students opportunities to formulate understandings about how fractions work. Many times students will begin a lesson with one understanding only to find that it needs to be readjusted and reevaluated as the lesson continues, given the nature of the activities and questions being asked.

OVERVIEW

Fractions (Grades 5–6)

Experiences at This Level Will Help Students To

- use different forms of representations such as physical models and drawings to reason about situations requiring the manipulation of fractions
- compare and order fractions
- use benchmarks that relate different forms of representations of rational numbers
- explore addition, subtraction, multiplication, and division of fractions
- use estimation to help make decisions
- develop methods for solving problems involving fractions

Reproducibles are available in a download-able, print-able format. See page xx for directions about how to access them.

Materials

- construction paper
- Cuisenaire rods
- pattern blocks
- pattern block templates
- Pattern Block Figure (Reproducible 2)
- Grid Figure (Reproducible 3)
- Fractions Dot Paper (Reproducible 4)
- 6-by-6-inch Template (Reproducible 5)
- scissors

Good Questions and Teacher Notes (pages 82–98)

GOOD QUESTIONS FOR MATH TEACHING   **81**

GOOD QUESTIONS AND TEACHER NOTES

> The following questions cover a variety of fraction concepts. Questions 1–9 address the topic of fraction models and Questions 10–12 focus on comparing fractions. With Question 13, the focus shifts to computation, specifically adding and subtracting fractions (Questions 13–17) and multiplying and dividing fractions (Questions 18–24).

 1. If the △ = 1, what is the value of the following shape?
   (See Reproducible 2, Pattern Block Figure.)

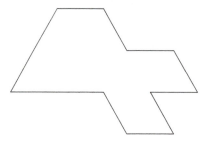

If the △ = $\frac{1}{4}$, what is the value of the preceding shape?

If the △ = $\frac{1}{2}$, what is the value of the preceding shape *now*?

Why do the same shapes keep switching values? Explain your reasoning with tracings of the pattern blocks and/or other diagrams.

Because of the given contexts (the value of the △), the value of the whole changes. This can be a very difficult and eye-opening concept for budding fraction aficionados! The whole matters. Understanding and being able to represent the whole becomes increasingly important as students are asked to make sense of their interpretations.

Pattern blocks are only one model that can be used to represent this big idea when studying fractions. (See the upcoming model question using Cuisenaire rods.)

FRACTIONS (GRADES 5–6)

2. If the blue rhombus equals $\frac{1}{4}$ create a shape with a value of $2\frac{1}{4}$. Sketch your construction and label each fractional part. Write an addition sentence that matches your construction on a sentence strip. Post the construction and turn in your addition sentence.

> Once the constructions and sentences have been completed, hold up an addition sentence and have the students match the sentence to its construction. This valuable exercise will reinforce the need for students to write what they see. Repeat this activity choosing different shapes and assigning different values. Make sure to try them out first yourself!

3. Estimate the solution for each of the following questions. Do NOT apply a computational strategy! Use a visual model such as a drawing, a number line, a hundredths grid, a bar model, or an area model to support your estimation.

   What is $\frac{1}{4}$ of 16?

   What is $\frac{3}{4}$ of 16?

   What is $\frac{2}{9}$ of 3?

   What is $\frac{2}{9}$ of 18?

   What is $\frac{1}{3}$ of 21?

   What is $\frac{2}{3}$ of 21?

> These questions explore the *set model* of fractional reasoning and thinking. As other problems are created, look to connect whole numbers, denominators, or numerators in some way. Encouraging students to apply what they learned from one problem to the next will strengthen their reasoning and problem-solving skills and confidence.

GOOD QUESTIONS FOR MATH TEACHING

GOOD QUESTIONS AND TEACHER NOTES

 4. **What fractional part of this square is shaded in? How do you know? Demonstrate a strategy to identify the fractional part shaded in.**

(See Reproducible 3, Grid Figure.)

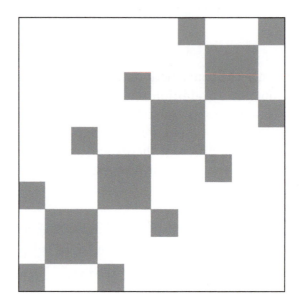

> Visual representations can anchor understanding. Creating designs that match constraints—color in $\frac{1}{3}$ of the square (or $\frac{5}{8}$ or $\frac{19}{20}$)—can support fractional awareness and estimation skills. Words such as *less*, *some*, or *more* in addition to a facility with benchmark fractions can move students to very accurate estimations. Posting equivalent fraction diagrams/representations can support meaningful classroom conversations about estimation strategies and equivalence.
>
> This activity can lend itself quite well to fraction to decimal to percent conversations as well. Using 10-by-10 grids will allow for easier conversions—but allow the students to make that realization on their own!

FRACTIONS (GRADES 5–6)

5. If the dark green Cuisinaire rod equals 1, what is the value of the following rods? Defend your position using the rods and what you know about fractional relationships.

red = _____   light green = _____   white = _____

Make trains of different-color Cuisinaire rods as indicated (see diagram that follows) and place them in front of you to help support your positions.

Dark Green					
Green			Green		
Red		Red		Red	
W	W	W	W	W	W

Create new trains as your value of the whole changes in order to answer the following questions:

orange = 1
red =
yellow =
white =

brown = 1
red =
purple =
white =

orange + red = 1
red =
light green =
dark green =
white =

As with the first pattern-block activity in the preceding section, this activity provides students with another model as they investigate the meaning of a whole and how that meaning impacts the naming of fractional parts. The visual model of the rods enables students to begin to reason about the relative size of fractional parts as well: that thirds are smaller than halves, fourths are larger than eighths, and so on.

As we teach for understanding, it is important to ask students to justify the thinking behind their statements. For example, *Why do you think the red rod is one-half? Why is the red rod one-half in this problem and not one-half in another problem?*

GOOD QUESTIONS FOR MATH TEACHING

GOOD QUESTIONS AND TEACHER NOTES

 6. Create your own fraction kit out of construction paper with halves, fourths, and sixteenths. What are the various strings of fractions that can add up to one whole? Can you find strings of three fractions? Four fractions? Five fractions? What is the longest string you can find that will add up to one whole? What is the shortest string? Write your strings as addition sentences (Burns 2015).

> The fraction kit offers yet another model for seeing fractional parts and representations. Writing strings ($\frac{1}{2} + \frac{1}{4} + \frac{1}{4} = 1$) offers students the opportunity to symbolically represent fractions. Informal conjectures about how adding works with fractions will also begin to develop when working with these strings.
>
> Adding strings of unlike denominators also gives students the opportunity to think through the numerical relationships of the given denominators. How are 2, 4, 8, and 16 related? What is the relationship of the numerator to the denominator? Because these fraction kits are so portable, homework assignments can easily be based on their usage.

FRACTIONS (GRADES 5–6)

 7. Using fractions dot paper, divide each square into fourths. Can you do this in more than one way? Explain.

(See Reproducible 4, Fractions Dot Paper.)

Students will quickly divide the whole into the common divisions of fourths. Instructional conversations will quickly ensue once the topic of irregular fourths, or shapes, is introduced, either by the teacher or by a student example.

"Are the pieces fourths if they do not look the same?" can be a powerful question. "Would each person get an equal amount if we were dividing up a pan of brownies? What constitutes equal?"

Encourage students to develop and articulate their strategies and reasoning for proving that noncongruent shapes can be equal. Show them the following diagram and ask: "Is this a fair division? How do you know?"

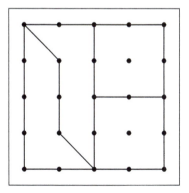

Using an area model, each region constitutes $\frac{1}{4}$.
$\frac{1}{4}$ of 16 units² = 4 units²
Each region equals 4 units².

Asking students to work with eighths within this same model can be an insightful follow-up activity in order to assess understanding and progress.

GOOD QUESTIONS FOR MATH TEACHING   87

GOOD QUESTIONS AND TEACHER NOTES

8. Use a 6-by-6-inch template to answer the following questions: How can you divide this square into halves, fourths, and eighths? Is there more than one way to divide up your square? Show your thinking on your diagram. Partition your square into halves, fourths, and eighths. Label and color-code each fractional part. Justify your divisions and labels.

(See Reproducible 5, 6-by-6-Inch Template.)

> Such an activity becomes more difficult without the use of dot paper. Rulers and even cutting out and folding the square can be useful. When students use rulers, rich conversations can develop around how to measure one-half of 3 inches or one-fourth of 6 inches.
>
> This same activity can be used to investigate and represent thirds, sixths, and twelfths.

9. Is this equation true or false? Support your thinking given any model discussed in class.

$$\frac{1}{2} = \frac{2}{3}$$

> Extending the use of such a question using other familiar fractions can solidify understanding. Have students articulate their reasoning in writing with the aid of diagrams as well as in a class discussion.
>
> Using unfamiliar fractions can develop new understandings based on what the students have already discovered about fractional parts. For example:
>
> $\frac{1}{15} < \frac{1}{16}$ *True or false? Why?*

FRACTIONS (GRADES 5–6)

 10. What patterns can you see in this series? How is each fraction related to the others? What do you notice about the third term? What do you notice about the fifth term? Can you predict the eleventh term?

$$\left\{\frac{1}{3}, \frac{2}{6}, \frac{3}{9}, \frac{4}{12}, \frac{5}{15}, \ldots\right\}$$

> Yes, these fractions are equivalent, but ask students to identify relationships between the fractions. Students may see the following:
>
> - As the numerator increases by one, the denominator increases by three.
> - The numerator increases more "slowly" than the denominator.
> - The third term has 3 as a numerator; the fifth term has 5; the eleventh term will have 11 as the numerator.
>
> Initially, choose patterns that begin with the *unit fraction* (a fraction with a numerator of 1). Moving on to patterns that start with fractions other than the unit fraction will help further develop students' understanding of *how* equivalent fractions can be generated and *how* they relate to one another.

 11. Use some of the digits 2, 3, 4, 5, 6, 7, and 8 to create fractions that could replace the missing values in this inequality:

$$? < ? < \frac{1}{2} < ?$$

> Excluding the digit 1 from the list of choices prevents students from using unit fractions and increases the complexity of the task.

GOOD QUESTIONS FOR MATH TEACHING

GOOD QUESTIONS AND TEACHER NOTES

12. Which one am I?

$$\frac{1}{2} \quad \frac{5}{12} \quad \frac{1}{4} \quad \frac{8}{10} \quad \frac{2}{3}$$

Clues:

I am less than one-half.

I am greater than one-third.

My denominator is a multiple of three. I am simplified.

I am _____.

Make up a fraction riddle with five fractions and clues for identifying one of them.

> A student's ability to compare and contrast fractions can demonstrate conceptual as well as procedural understanding. Creating riddles also allows students the opportunity to apply other numerical concepts to their clues.

13. Write a story problem that can be solved with this number sentence:

$$2\tfrac{1}{4} + \tfrac{1}{8} + 1\tfrac{1}{2} = 3\tfrac{7}{8}$$

Justify its solution as well. Use visual models and number sentences.

> Writing story problems can help teachers assess students' understanding or misconceptions. We can assess how the students are adding but also how they are making sense of the fractional relationships within the context of their stories. Asking students to write about subtraction models is as important as having them write about addition models.

FRACTIONS (GRADES 5–6)

14. If you add me to $\frac{3}{4}$, you end up with $\frac{7}{8}$. What fractional part am I? Demonstrate your solution with a visual model and/or number sentence. Can you demonstrate another way of solving this riddle?

> Students who have a good understanding of fractional relationships can very often be flexible in their thinking; for example, $\frac{3}{4} + ? = \frac{7}{8}$ or $\frac{7}{8} - \frac{3}{4} = ?$
>
> Fractional riddles such as this can help students apply what they already know about whole number operations to what they are learning about fractions. The formation of riddles can easily be applied to decimals, or even to both decimals and fractions in one riddle!

15. Using some of the digits from 1 through 8, place one digit in each box to satisfy the following: What is the least possible sum? What is the greatest possible sum? How did you go about making your number choices?

$$\frac{\square}{\square} + \frac{\square}{\square}$$

> This question not only asks students to add fractions but also to make judgments about the relative value of each fraction created. Students must also consider relationships between the numerators and denominators when placing the digits.

GOOD QUESTIONS FOR MATH TEACHING   91

GOOD QUESTIONS AND TEACHER NOTES

 16. Estimate the sums of the following expressions WITHOUT computing common denominators! Support your thinking with the decomposition of addends or visual models such as open number lines.

$$\frac{1}{2} + \frac{5}{8}$$

$$\frac{1}{2} + \frac{4}{5}$$

$$\frac{5}{9} + \frac{3}{27}$$

$$\frac{2}{3} + \frac{5}{15}$$

Just as students have explored the commutative property, the decomposition of addends, and the use of open number line procedures with whole numbers, they can extend and apply these strategies to the addition of fractions. The process of addition does not change whether the numbers are whole or rational.

An understanding of fractional equivalence is also hugely helpful as students estimate sums. A possible solution for $\frac{1}{2} + \frac{5}{8}$ could be:

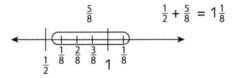

Additional support and ideas for instruction can be found in *Beyond Invert and Multiply* (McNamara 2015). This is an excellent instructional resource that can and will support student's fractional number sense and ground procedural proficiency in conceptual understanding.

FRACTIONS (GRADES 5–6)

 17. $\frac{1}{a} - \frac{1}{b} = \frac{1}{c}$

Find three different numbers for the denominators that will make this a true sentence. Can you find another set of numbers that will work?

> Initially, students may employ a guess-and-check procedure. Some students will also be convinced that this sentence will be false no matter what numbers are chosen. Asking students to focus on common denominators can help open up thinking and reasoning. Once students have decided on a set of numbers, have them test their fractions within the given equation. Calculation practice takes on meaning and purpose when presented in a problem-solving context.

 18. Before asking the question, draw seven circles on the board. If you had seven cookies to divide up among four people, how could you do it? How many cookies—or what part of a cookie—would each person get? Write your solution as an addition fraction string that equals 7.

> It is important for the students to represent their divisions symbolically. Initially, it may not be a formalized number sentence. Partitioning cookies and then labeling their parts is a common and very helpful approach. Ask students to formalize their solutions into number sentences once they have made sense of their divisions and reasons for doing so. Students should be encouraged to prove their thinking and to justify their reasoning to you, each other, and/or in writing.
>
> You can extend this question by sharing four cookies with six people or sharing eight cookies with five people. Dividing brownies (squares) can give students another model with which to test their procedures and understanding.

GOOD QUESTIONS FOR MATH TEACHING

GOOD QUESTIONS AND TEACHER NOTES

19. I have twenty-four coins in my pocket.

- One-half of the coins are quarters.
- One-fourth of the coins are dimes.
- One-eighth of the coins are nickels.
- One-eighth of the coins are pennies.

How much money do I have in my pocket? How did you come to this conclusion? Describe your thinking. How would you have changed your procedure if the amount of money were known and you were asked how many coins I had in my pocket?

Multiple manipulations are necessary in solving coin riddles such as these. There are also multiple methods of finding solutions, which makes these riddles interesting and entertaining to process. Some may utilize a guess-and-check procedure and others may opt for an algebraic computation method.

Having students make up their own riddles, as well as describing their procedures for creating and solving them, can be a useful extension. It may be necessary to model how to devise a coin riddle as a class activity, keeping in mind that the fractional parts listed need to be components of one whole (the amount of money or the number of coins). It is not an easy procedure!

FRACTIONS (GRADES 5–6)

 20. Annie is a great babysitter. She makes $6.50 an hour. Dava is an even better babysitter. She makes $2\frac{1}{2}$ times more than Annie per hour.

How much does Dava make per hour?

How much more does Dava make than Annie per hour?

How many hours does Annie need to babysit before she can equal Dava's pay for two hours of babysitting?

> The relational language in multiplicative comparison problems (*times as many*, *times more*) is difficult for many students. Students will often decide to add or subtract, confusing *times more* with *more than*. Presenting story problems based on relational comparisons will help students identify the appropriate operation.
>
> Problems that include both fractions and decimals present contextual situations that require students to make problem-solving choices. Can the student manipulate both in the same problem? Is it necessary to convert one to the other? Which form makes more sense given the context—or does it really matter?

 21. When you multiply two whole numbers, the product is larger than the factors. When is the product of two fractions smaller than the fractions being multiplied? Explain your reasoning and give examples to support your thinking.

> When multiplying fractions that are less than 1, you are taking a part of something that itself is part of a whole. The product can, therefore, *not* be bigger than either of the two fractions. This can be very confusing to students who have come to believe that multiplication makes something bigger.

GOOD QUESTIONS FOR MATH TEACHING 95

GOOD QUESTIONS AND TEACHER NOTES

 22. Can you find a fraction and a whole number with a product that is a whole number?

Can you find a fraction and a whole number with a product less than $\frac{1}{2}$?

Can you find a fraction and a whole number with a product greater than 1?

Can you find a fraction and a whole number with a product greater than $1\frac{1}{2}$ but less than 2?

Explain your method for choosing and checking possible solutions.

> Questions such as these can offer students more meaningful calculation practice than a sheet of multiplication problems! Reasoning skills, as well as procedural proficiency, are necessary to test and identify solutions. You may also find that students will complete many more calculations as they search for fractions and whole numbers that will produce the desired products. Asking students to test solutions offered by you or student volunteers can also provide further calculating practice.

FRACTIONS (GRADES 5–6)

 23. **When dividing fractions, can your answer be greater than, less than, or between the two fractions you are dividing? Explain why or why not for each situation and give examples to illustrate your position.**

> The answer to all three is yes, which will surprise many students. Some will automatically assume that the answer will always be *less than* the original fractions because to divide is often equated with making something smaller.
>
> It may be necessary for you to model a situation for each solution, and it will be well worth the time. Though not all students will walk away saying, "Oh yes, I see," at the very least, students will walk away with an understanding that dividing with fractions does not always denote making them smaller.
>
> > The answer can be *greater* than the fractions you are dividing: $\frac{3}{4} \div \frac{1}{4} = 3$, which means that there are three one-fourths in three-fourths.
> >
> > The answer can be *smaller* than the fractions you are dividing: $\frac{3}{4} \div 2 = \frac{3}{8}$, which means that if $\frac{3}{4}$ is the size of 2 groups, $\frac{3}{8}$ is the size of one group.
>
> Dividing a fraction by a whole number is the same as multiplying it by its reciprocal. The reciprocal is a number less than one, which brings us back to the question of what happens when you multiply two fractions.
>
> > The answer can be *in between*: $\frac{1}{4} \div \frac{3}{4} = \frac{1}{3}$. If the problem is rewritten with common denominators, the relationship is easier to see: $\frac{3}{12} \div \frac{9}{12} = \frac{4}{12}$.

GOOD QUESTIONS FOR MATH TEACHING   97

GOOD QUESTIONS AND TEACHER NOTES

 24. Suppose that Max, the wonder dog, ate one-third of a bag of doggie treats on Sunday night. Max then proceeded to eat one-fourth of what remained in the bag every night after that. How many nights would it take until the bag was half gone? Could you determine when it would be time to buy Max another bag of doggie treats? Draw a diagram to support your solutions.

> Using array diagrams can be helpful to students as they work to determine when the bag was half gone. The bag would be half gone by Monday night.
>
> | Mon. | Mon. | Sun. |
> |------|------|------|
> | | | Sun. |
> | | | Sun. |
> | | | Sun. |
>
> After Monday, six out of the twelve parts are gone.
>
> Responses to the second question (when will it be time to buy another bag?) is subject to the individual opinions of the students. Will the bag ever be empty? Can you theoretically ever have an empty bag if you are forever taking one-quarter of what is left?
>
> This problem can also be reworked using percentages. In that case, a pie chart may be a better visual representation.

OVERVIEW

DECIMALS (GRADES 5–6)

EXPERIENCES AT THIS LEVEL WILL HELP STUDENTS TO

- use different forms of representations such as physical models and drawings to reason about situations requiring the manipulation of decimal numbers
- compare and order decimals
- use benchmarks that relate different representations of rational numbers
- explore addition, subtraction, multiplication, and division of decimal numbers
- use estimation to make decisions
- develop methods for solving problems involving fractions and decimal numbers

Reproducibles are available in a downloadable, printable format. See page xx for directions about how to access them.

MATERIALS

- Tenths and Hundredths Grid (Reproducible 6)
- Hundredths Grid (Reproducible 7)
- meter sticks, centimeter cubes (orange and white Cuisenaire rods work well)

GOOD QUESTIONS AND TEACHER NOTES (PAGES 100–109)

GOOD QUESTIONS FOR MATH TEACHING   **99**

GOOD QUESTIONS AND TEACHER NOTES

> The following questions cover a variety of decimal concepts. While Questions 1–7 provide an introduction to decimal concepts, the remaining questions dive into decimal computation. Questions 8–12 focus on adding and subtracting decimals and Questions 13–17 focus on multiplying and dividing fractions.

1. Decide whether each decimal is closer to 0, $\frac{1}{2}$, or 1. Shade in the decimal amounts on a tenths or hundredths grid to justify your thinking.

    (See Reproducible 6, Tenths and Hundredths Grid.)

    0.2   0.55   0.03   0.4   0.09   0.90   0.6   0.75

> Benchmark decimals and fractions can serve as useful reference points. Being able to identify the relative value of decimals can help students make better comparisons between decimals and fractions. Asking the follow-up question, "How do you know?" once an answer is given allows the teacher to hear students' understandings or misconceptions.
>
> You may also want to add one-fourth and three-fourths to your benchmarks as students become more comfortable with this activity. They may also ask to include these benchmarks!

DECIMALS (GRADES 5–6)

2. **Mrs. Flo Wer is planting a garden. She wants to follow the plans listed here:**

   Flo wants four-tenths of the garden to be planted with geraniums.

   Flo wants fifteen-hundredths of the garden to be planted with marigolds.

   Flo wants three-tenths of the garden to be planted with tulips.

   Flo wants the remaining sections of her garden to be planted with sunflowers and daisies.

   Use a hundredths grid to "plant" Mrs. Flo Wer's garden. Then complete the following chart with the fraction and decimal equivalent of the garden space that will be allotted to each kind of flower in your plan.

   (See Reproducible 7, Hundredths Grid.)

Flower	Fraction	Decimal

   Adding a column for percentage notation is also a possibility. This type of visual model lends itself well to a discussion of percentage.

   Why do some students' gardens look different than others? Are they "correct," given Flo's requirements? Explain your position.

GOOD QUESTIONS FOR MATH TEACHING

GOOD QUESTIONS AND TEACHER NOTES

 3. Using these units of measure:

meter

decimeter

centimeter

How could you represent 2.17? How could you represent 0.9? How could you represent 0.28? Using these measures, how can you prove that 0.3 = 0.30? What would one-thousandth look like?

> This measurement model can be helpful when students are working to make sense of the multiplicative relationship between decimal place values. Defining the root *deci-* of *decimal* can also help highlight the relationship.

 4. Where do the following decimals fit? How do you know?

0.86   0.2   0.99   0.49   0.75   0.01   0.6

0 — — — — — — —0.5— — — — — —1.0

> It is important to give students multiple opportunities to talk about order and equivalence in regard to decimals. Having access to tenths and hundredths grid paper may be helpful to some as they explain their thinking. Assign this question for homework with the addition of fractions!

DECIMALS (GRADES 5–6)

5. Mark and label a point for a decimal number that fits each description that follows.

1——————————————————————2

a point close to, but larger than 1

a point close to, but smaller than $\frac{1}{2}$

a point close to, but larger than $1\frac{1}{2}$

a point close to, but smaller than 2

As with fractions, it is important for students to see decimals in multiple representations. Using number lines can offer students a continuum on which to see quantity and equivalence.

6. Solve this riddle:

1 _._ _ _

Clue 1: The digit in the hundredths place is double the digit in the tenths place.

Clue 2: The digit in the tenths place is odd.

Clue 3: The digit in the thousandths place represents the sum of the digits in the tenths place and hundredths place.

Clue 4: The digit in the ones place is four times the digit in the hundredths place.

Number riddles can provide a context within which to review and solidify place-value understandings. The spelling alone (adding the ever important -ths to decimal places) of the place values is important! Extend this question by having students make up their own riddles.

GOOD QUESTIONS FOR MATH TEACHING

GOOD QUESTIONS AND TEACHER NOTES

 7. True or false?

$\frac{1}{2} = 0.5$

Are these two quantities equal or equivalent? How do you know? Justify your thinking with a diagram or drawing.

> Some may argue that these two specific *written representations* are not equal because they do not look the same. They do, however, represent the same *value*, which makes them equivalent. This idea of equivalence is extremely important in the study of mathematics. Conversations around it can be rich and insightful. Ask students to write about equivalence as well. Change the numbers (example: $\frac{3}{4} = 0.75$) to see if the concept is conserved!

 8. Write pairs of decimals to complete each column in the table.

Sums

Greater Than 1	Equal To 1	Less Than 1
0.76 + 0.44	0.55 + 0.45	0.2 + 0.35

Explain how you can tell whether the sum of two decimals will be greater than 1.
Explain how you can tell whether the sum of two decimals will be less than 1.
Explain how you can tell whether the sum of two decimals will be equal to 1.

> As students try to understand how decimals work, it is important to give them opportunities to formulate ideas of how decimal numbers operate. It is equally important for them to talk *and* write about these understandings.

DECIMALS (GRADES 5–6)

 9. Write pairs of decimals to complete each column in the table.

Differences

Greater Than 1	Equal To 1	Less Than 1
3.5 – 0.4	2.65 – 1.65	0.88 – 0.7

Explain how you can tell whether the difference of two decimals will be greater than 1.
Explain how you can tell whether the difference of two decimals will be less than 1.
Explain how you can tell whether the difference of two decimals will be equal to 1.

Comparing and contrasting the operations of addition and subtraction can provide meaningful instruction. Activities such as this also allow students opportunities to develop estimating strategies to approximate particular sums or differences.

---

 10. Suppose you know the answer to Problem A. How can you use what you know about Problem A to solve Problem B? Solve both problems. Was your assumption correct?

```
PROBLEM A      PROBLEM B
  72.15          72.15
 -23.79         -43.79
```

Too often students rely solely on computation to assess the reasonableness of an answer. The ability to estimate is powerful and useful. Estimating the magnitude of one answer by using information available from another can be an effective strategy.

Offering students opportunities to predict results and to identify patterns of calculations is important. Try a similar approach with addition of decimals.

GOOD QUESTIONS FOR MATH TEACHING

GOOD QUESTIONS AND TEACHER NOTES

11. Write a story problem with an answer of 12.2. Your problem should require the addition of three numbers.

> Giving a context to a calculation can be difficult. It not only requires a degree of mastery with the procedure but also an understanding of how the numbers need to relate to one another. Much addition and even subtraction practice will result from such an activity as the students work to identify numbers that will adhere to the constraints of the given problem.

12. Work with the digit sets 1234 and 987.

    You may insert a decimal point just before, between, or after each given set of digits.

    You cannot change the order of the digits.

    You may add zeros only if they do not change the value of your number.

    Find ways to insert the decimal points so that you can get five different sums using these two sets of digits. What is the largest sum that you can make? What is the smallest sum?

> Students can often generalize their understanding of addition with whole numbers to addition with decimal numbers. The requirement of manipulating the decimal points allows students the opportunity to make important generalizations about how, when, and where decimal points in numbers affect sums.

DECIMALS (GRADES 5–6)

 13. The mean of a set of four numbers is 5. Two of the numbers are 4.3 and 8.15. What might be the other two numbers?

> Division as well as addition and estimation proficiency are required by such a question. You could ask follow-up questions such as: "What would you have to do to the data set to get a *higher* mean? A *lower* mean? How would the data set be different if you needed to add three numbers?"

 14. Which of the following problems has the largest product? Try to figure it out by solving as few of the problems as possible.

$$3.2 \times 17 \quad 50 \times 3.5 \quad 1.7 \times 50$$
$$24 \times 2.9 \quad 2.4 \times 29 \quad 5.0 \times 36$$

> The ability to assess and estimate the magnitude of products will help students determine which numbers to try. Important calculation practice is often hidden when students are working to solve an intriguing problem.

GOOD QUESTIONS FOR MATH TEACHING   107

GOOD QUESTIONS AND TEACHER NOTES

 15. Can you create a problem in which the product of two decimals is smaller than either of the numbers being multiplied? What was your strategy?

Possible solution: 0.14 × 0.4 = 0.056. When two numbers less than one are multiplied, the product will be smaller than both of the numbers.

A great deal of multiplication practice will be carried out as students work to find decimal numbers that will adhere to the constraints of this problem. Finding one solution may not allow the students to make generalizations about their findings. It may be necessary to encourage students to find multiple solutions before they make conjectures.

 16. Can you create a problem in which the product of two decimals is larger than either of the numbers multiplied? What was your strategy?

Possible solution: 1.6 × 1.7 = 2.72. When two numbers greater than one are multiplied, the product will be greater than both of the numbers. If one of the numbers is less than 1 and the other is greater than 1, the product will be larger than only *one* of the numbers.

Understanding how multiplication affects the products of various types of decimal numbers allows students to make sense of the rules that govern multiplication computations. Such an understanding can enable students to make more accurate estimates and assess the reasonableness of computations.

DECIMALS (GRADES 5–6)

 17. Create a story problem with a quotient of 3.4. Solve your story problem. How did you go about choosing your numbers?

> Having students create story problems can give teachers a lens through which to view students' conceptual as well as procedural understandings. Being given the solution and then being asked to work backward can be a challenge for some. It is often the conceptual understanding, or lack of such, that can cause difficulties with a task like this. It requires careful reading on the teacher's part to assess the accuracy and appropriateness of a context. Assign story problems requiring different constraints, operations, or even multiple operations.

OVERVIEW

PERCENTAGES (Grades 5–6)

Experiences at This Level Will Help Students To

- move comfortably between differing representations of rational numbers
- compare and order rational numbers
- use benchmarks that relate different forms of representations of rational numbers
- develop methods for solving problems involving rational numbers
- use estimation to help make decisions

Reproducibles are available in a downloadable, printable format. See page xx for directions about how to access them.

Materials

- Hundredths Grid (Reproducible 7)
- calculators
- sale flyers from local newspaper

Good Questions and Teacher Notes (pages 111–114)

110   GOOD QUESTIONS FOR MATH TEACHING

PERCENTAGES (GRADES 5–6)

1. How can you change a percentage to a fraction?

   A percentage to a decimal?

   A decimal to a fraction? A decimal to a percentage?

   A fraction to a decimal?

   A fraction to a percentage?

   Give a numerical example and a written explanation for each situation and use drawings when you can.

   > It becomes increasingly important for students to be able to move flexibly among the representations of fractions, decimals, and percentages. Using friendly-denominator fractions (factors of a hundred) can help solidify concepts of equivalence as students move from one to the other.

2. Using hundredths grids, shade in the following amounts. Write equivalent representations using a fraction and a decimal.

   (See Reproducible 7, Hundredths Grid.)

   50%   25%   75%   80%

   > Using an area model can help students make sense of the multiple representations of the same quantity.

GOOD QUESTIONS FOR MATH TEACHING   111

GOOD QUESTIONS AND TEACHER NOTES

3. Place these fractions, decimals, and percentages on a number line. Use a different number line for each set of numbers. Explain the reasoning of your placement of each number.

   25%, 1.55, $\frac{2}{3}$, 75%

   $\frac{1}{4}$, 1.49, 88%, 45%

   0.05, 0.5, 50%, 0.55

   $0 - - - - \frac{1}{2} - - - - 1 - - - - 1\frac{1}{2} - - - - 2$

> Order counts! This activity can serve students well if the follow-up is done as a class discussion. Such a forum can be used to push the clarity of students' thinking and language.

4. *California* has ten letters.

   What fraction of the state name is made up of vowels? Write this fraction as a decimal.

   What percentage of the state name is made up of consonants?

   What fraction of the state name is made up of the letter A?

   What percentage of the state name is made up of the letter C? Write these percentages as decimals.

   Can you name a state of which more than 50 percent of its letters are vowels?

> These conversions may not be so neat and tidy. Instruction on rounding can be more meaningful and useful when applied in a problem-solving context. Calculator usage may be an option once conceptual understanding of how conversions work is established. Asking students to create their own state riddles and conversion questions can help support the thinking required to move flexibly between fractions, decimals, and percentage.

PERCENTAGES (GRADES 5–6)

 5. Pure Hockey is having a sale of 30 percent off all junior shin guards.

If CCM shin guards sell for $64.99, what is the amount of discount? What is the new sale price after the discount?

If Bauer shin guards sell for $49.99, what is the amount of discount? What is the new sale price after the discount?

If I have $55.25 in my wallet, which shin guards can I buy on sale with a 5 percent sales tax?

Show your thinking and calculations.

Discount problems are popular in most textbooks—and practical because of their real-life application. It is important, however, to ask a series of varied questions. What is the discount? What is the new price? How much more money will I need to make a purchase?

Using sales flyers from newspapers can offer opportunities for continued meaningful application. Students can create their own percentage questions within constraints set by the teacher or class given the prices on a flyer.

GOOD QUESTIONS FOR MATH TEACHING

GOOD QUESTIONS AND TEACHER NOTES

 6. Alissa and Nadia conducted a survey of the students in their mathematics class. They found out the following information:

75 percent of the students in the class do homework three or more nights each week. Of the students who do homework three or more nights a week, half do homework five nights each week.

From the information given, can you tell how many students are in the class? Explain why or why not.

Percentages represent *comparisons*, not exact quantities. Therefore, students *cannot* tell how many are in the class given the information presented. Ask students to present different possible answers. For example: If there are forty kids in the class, thirty kids do homework three or more nights. Of those thirty kids, fifteen do homework five nights a week.

OVERVIEW

FRACTIONS (GRADES 7–8)

EXPERIENCES AT THIS LEVEL WILL HELP STUDENTS TO

- order and compare positive and negative fractions
- convert fractions into decimals and percentages
- represent addition and subtraction of rational numbers on a number line
- recognize situations that call for the multiplication and division of rational numbers
- add, subtract, multiply, and divide rational numbers
- estimate the results of computations involving fractions

Reproducibles are available in a downloadable, printable format. See page xx for directions about how to access them.

MATERIALS

- calculators
- Graph Paper (Reproducible A)

GOOD QUESTIONS AND TEACHER NOTES (PAGES 116–120)

GOOD QUESTIONS FOR MATH TEACHING   **115**

GOOD QUESTIONS AND TEACHER NOTES

 1. Find a fraction that is less than $-\frac{1}{100}$ but greater than $-\frac{2}{100}$.

Once students identify a possible fraction, ask them to estimate the location of their fraction on a number line. Be sure to talk about why $-\frac{1}{100}$ is greater than $-\frac{2}{100}$ (even though $\frac{1}{100}$ is less than $\frac{2}{100}$).

 2. Louisa put a list of fractions, decimals, and percentages in order from least to greatest by converting all numbers to percentages and putting the percentages in order from least to greatest. But she then forgot to write the numbers in their original forms. What might the original numbers have been?

-62.5% < -0.5% < 75% < 80% < 160%

The most obvious answer can be found by converting the percentages to fractions with denominators that are powers of 10. By looking beyond this answer and investigating other equivalents, however, students will develop facility with common fraction-decimal-percentage conversions.

 3. Estimate the location of each point on the number line.

Make sure students refer to their answers as signed numbers or rational numbers and not integers.

GOOD QUESTIONS FOR MATH TEACHING

FRACTIONS (GRADES 7–8)

 4. Two rational numbers, *a* and *b*, have a sum of $-3\frac{1}{4}$. Neither *a* nor *b* is an integer. What might be the values of *a* and *b*?

You can create additional variations of this question by changing the operation (e.g., two rational numbers, *a* and *b*, have a difference of $-3\frac{1}{4}$).

 5. Give the length and width of a rectangle with an area that measures a little more than 24 square units.

Some students might benefit from sketching possible solutions on graph paper. (See Reproducible A, Graph Paper.) As students work, look to see whether they apply what they know about solving whole number area problems to find the length and width of the room.

 6. Frank looked at a fraction division computation and said, "I know the answer will be a whole number." What might have been the computation? What do you think Frank noticed?

The repeated subtraction interpretation of division can be helpful here. For example, $4 \div \frac{1}{4}$ can be interpreted as the number of groups of $\frac{1}{4}$ in 4; $4 \div \frac{1}{4} = 16$. Or, $\frac{2}{3} \div \frac{1}{3}$ can be read as the number of groups of $\frac{1}{3}$ in $\frac{2}{3}$; $\frac{2}{3} \div \frac{1}{3} = 2$.

GOOD QUESTIONS FOR MATH TEACHING   117

GOOD QUESTIONS AND TEACHER NOTES

7. The mixed numbers in the following problem are missing. Use the partial products to find the two mixed numbers.

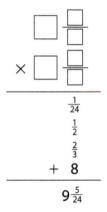

> Help students make the connection between the partial-product method for multiplying two-digit whole numbers and the partial-product method for multiplying mixed numbers. Also, after students find different solutions to the problem, encourage them to find connections between them.

8. Eugenio estimated the answer to a fraction multiplication computation by finding half of a number close to 8. What might have been the computation?

> Since Eugenio is using estimation, it is not necessary for one fraction to be exactly equal to $\frac{1}{2}$. Instead, this fraction can be close to $\frac{1}{2}$. For example, $\frac{4}{9} \times 8\frac{1}{10}$ is similar to taking half of a number close to 8.

GOOD QUESTIONS FOR MATH TEACHING

FRACTIONS (GRADES 7–8)

9. Two rational numbers, *a* and *b*, have a product that is less than -8 but greater than -9. What might be the values of *a* and *b*?

> One way to answer this question is to find two integers with a product of -8 (e.g., -4 × 2) and then find a rational number close to one of the factors such that product is less than -8 (e.g., -4.1 × 2 or 4 × -2.1).

10. Use the following rational numbers to fill in the missing values in the inequalities below. Do not compute to find your answers.

    $-12\frac{1}{2}$, $-\frac{11}{12}$, 45.98, 0.24

    __ (__ − __) > 0

    __ (__ − __) < 0

> One way to answer this equation is to reason about the signs of the factors. For example, the inequality __ (__ − __) > 0 can be thought of as a product of two factors (where the second factor is expressed as a difference). Since we want the product to be positive, we need to create two negative factors (e.g., $-\frac{11}{12}(-12\frac{1}{2} - 0.24) > 0$).

GOOD QUESTIONS FOR MATH TEACHING

GOOD QUESTIONS AND TEACHER NOTES

 11. One of the numbers in the following inequality has been erased. Find a number that could make a true inequality.

$$\frac{3}{\frac{1}{4}} > 3 \div \underline{}$$

This question encourages students to connect fractions to division. If we think of the expression on the left as a division, we can interpret it as the number of groups of $\frac{1}{4}$ that can be repeatedly subtracted from 3. Looking at the expression on the right, any number greater than $\frac{1}{4}$ will result in a smaller value.

 12. What might be the missing fraction in the following equation so that the value of x is an integer?

$$\frac{?}{?}x = 12$$

Observe students as they work to see if they can rely on mental math to find a possible answer. For example, one possible answer is $\frac{1}{4}x = 12$, which can be interpreted as one-fourth of a number, x, is 12. To find the value of x, we multiply 12×4 to get 48.

GOOD QUESTIONS FOR MATH TEACHING

OVERVIEW

DECIMALS (GRADES 7–8)

EXPERIENCES AT THIS LEVEL WILL HELP STUDENTS TO

- order and compare decimals with other representations of rational numbers
- understand the relationships between terminating and nonterminating decimals
- convert positive and negative decimals into fractions and percentages and vice versa
- use positive and negative decimals to represent the result of a division
- understand that all rational numbers can be written as decimals but not all decimals are rational numbers
- add, subtract, multiply, and divide decimals
- estimate the results of computations involving decimals

MATERIALS

- calculators

GOOD QUESTIONS AND TEACHER NOTES (PAGES 122–125)

GOOD QUESTIONS FOR MATH TEACHING   121

GOOD QUESTIONS AND TEACHER NOTES

 1. Juana is 5.6 feet tall and Jeremy is 5.8 feet tall. Liza is taller than Juana but shorter than Jeremy. How tall might she be in feet and inches?

> This question is designed to address the misconception that 5.6 feet is equivalent to 5 feet and 6 inches. If students believe this misconception, they might answer that Liza could be 5 feet and 7 inches tall, which is not correct. To address this misconception, ask students to express 5.5 or $5\frac{1}{2}$ feet using feet and inches.

 2. Replace the question marks with rational numbers to create a true equation:

$-0.25 = ? \div ? = \frac{?}{?}$

> This question encourages students to connect fractions, decimals, and division and understand equivalence between rational numbers less than 0 (e.g., $-1 \div 4 = 1 \div -4 = \frac{-1}{4} = \frac{1}{-4} = -\frac{1}{4}$).

 3. Fill in the blanks in the following sentence using some of these terms: *terminating decimals, repeating decimals, nonterminating decimals, nonrepeating decimals, rational numbers,* or *irrational numbers*. (You may use the same term more than once in one sentence.)

All _____ are _____, but not all _____ are _____.

> As students formulate answers to this question, listen for common misconceptions including the idea that repeating decimals are irrational numbers and nonterminating decimals are always repeating decimals.

DECIMALS (GRADES 7–8)

4. Place one integer, one rational number, and one irrational number on the number line below.

This question provides a context for students to make sense of repeating decimals as points on a number line. Be sure to ask students whether the number $5.\overline{742}$ is rational or irrational.

5. RJ's teacher asked him to determine if the number $\frac{14}{17}$ was rational or irrational. RJ used his calculator to compute 14 ÷ 17 and the number "0.823529412" appeared on the screen. RJ said, "It doesn't look like the decimal repeats, so $\frac{14}{17}$ must be an irrational number." Do you agree or disagree with RJ's answer?

Some students mistake a decimal with a long repetend with an irrational number. By definition, the number $\frac{14}{17}$ is rational because it is written as a ratio of two integers ($\frac{a}{b}$ where $b \neq 0$).

6. When you look at a fraction, how can you tell whether its decimal equivalent will terminate or not?

This is a very complex question that will likely require a lot of class time to discuss. One way to answer this question is to generate lists of fractions whose decimal representations repeat or terminate and look for generalizations. For more information on this topic, see *Math Matters* (Chapin and Johnson 2000).

GOOD QUESTIONS FOR MATH TEACHING 123

GOOD QUESTIONS AND TEACHER NOTES

7. The volume of a rectangular shipping box is 4.125 cubic feet. What might the dimensions be?

One way students might solve this problem is to convert 4.125 to $4\frac{1}{8}$ and find three numbers with that product.

8. A three-digit number was multiplied by a four-digit number to get a number close to 10. What might these numbers have been?

One possible answer is 2.47 × 4.012. By answering this question, students will learn that it is the relative size of decimal numbers and not simply their number of digits that is most helpful in estimating their product.

9. In the following problem, the decimal points were accidentally erased from the two numbers. Looking at the answer, what do you think the two numbers were?

```
    145
   x 46
   ────
    870
 + 5800
   ────
  6.670
```

Trying to multiply every combination of decimal numbers is not an efficient way of answering this question. Instead, students should try to interpret the problem using what they know about multiplication and estimation.

124   GOOD QUESTIONS FOR MATH TEACHING

DECIMALS (GRADES 7–8)

10. Wanda looked at a decimal computation in her math book and said, "This is kind of like taking a third of a number that is close to one." Create a computation that fits this description.

> Being able to interpret a decimal multiplication computation helps students solve the computation. It is of particular importance in judging the reasonableness of an answer.

11. I divided two decimals and got a quotient that was one hundred times greater than the dividend. What numbers might I have divided?

> After sharing students' answers, ask them why the quotient is greater than the dividend. If students seem confused by this question, prompt them to apply the repeated-subtraction interpretation of division to their computations (e.g., The computation 2.3 ÷ 0.01 can be thought of as the number of groups of one-hundredths that are in 2.3. Since there are 100 one-hundredths per whole, the answer will be 100 times greater than the dividend; 2.3 ÷ 0.01 = 230).

GOOD QUESTIONS FOR MATH TEACHING

OVERVIEW

PERCENTAGES (GRADES 7–8)

EXPERIENCES AT THIS LEVEL WILL HELP STUDENTS TO

- interpret percentages as comparisons to one hundred
- make sense of percentages greater than one hundred
- compare percentages with other forms of rational numbers and other types of numbers
- solve problems about percentage increase and decrease
- select appropriate operations when solving percentage problems

MATERIALS

- optional: calculators

GOOD QUESTIONS AND TEACHER NOTES (PAGES 127–131)

PERCENTAGES (GRADES 7–8)

1. Use the digits 0, 1, 2, 3, 4, 5, 6, 7, 8, 9 exactly one time each to create numbers that fit this ordering:

   fraction < decimal < fraction < positive integer < percentage

   > In order to answer this question correctly, students will need to create a percentage greater than one hundred, a concept they often struggle with.

2. The chance of rain, a sales discount, a likelihood of winning a carnival game, and the part of a dollar as written on a check were all equal but written in different ways. What might the different ways be? (National Council of Teachers of Mathematics 2000)

   > Although there are infinitely many possibilities, students' choices should make sense in the given contexts.

3. A jewelry store is planning a "sale." It wants to offer 25 percent off its jewelry prices but have the customer pay just as much for the jewelry as if it were not on sale. How can this be done?

   > Insist that students say more than, "The store increases its prices before the sale." Instead, require that students quantify such a statement by giving the percent of increase and justifying their answers with several examples.

GOOD QUESTIONS FOR MATH TEACHING

GOOD QUESTIONS AND TEACHER NOTES

4. A bag of jelly beans reads, "Now 33% more jelly beans in every bag!" How many jelly beans might have been in a bag and how many might be in a bag now?

> For homework, ask students to bring in food labels that advertise similar percentage increases.

5. Joan's parents bought her a basketball hoop for her birthday. As a result, her free-throw average has increased 110 percent. What might her average have been and what might it be now?

> Observing as students explore percentages greater than 100 will give you keen insight into their understanding of percentage as a *comparison* with 100 instead of as a fraction of 100.

6. Ligaya moved to a new house in her town. Her bus ride is now 20 minutes shorter than it used to be. How long might Ligaya's bus ride have been, and given this time, by what percentage has her ride time decreased?

> Once students find a possible answer, ask them to describe Ligaya's shortened bus ride using language associated with fractions or multiplicative reasoning.

PERCENTAGES (GRADES 7–8)

7. Carl's average on four tests in math was 89.5 percent, but his percentage score on each test was a whole number. What might have been Carl's test scores?

> One way to solve this problem is to find the product of 89.5 and 4. This would give the total of Carl's tests scores which can then be split into four different test scores.

8. Hoai calculated her test average after the first three tests of the school year. If she earns a 90 percent on tomorrow's math test, her average will increase to 85 percent. What scores might Hoai have earned on her first three tests?

> Students may answer that Hoai earned 80 percent on each of her first three tests. They may reason that this would result in a new average of 85 percent since the average of 80 percent and 90 percent is 85 percent. This answer is incorrect, however, because it does not give enough weight to her current average, which is based on three test scores.

9. A pollster found that exactly $36.\overline{6}$ percent of people prefer two-door cars to four-door cars. How many people might have been surveyed?

> Do students know how to interpret tenths of percentages? Do students think of using equivalent ratios to solve this problem?

GOOD QUESTIONS FOR MATH TEACHING

GOOD QUESTIONS AND TEACHER NOTES

10. A newspaper featured ads for sales on baseball hats at two different stores. The ad for one store read, "Buy 1 get 1 free." The ad for the other store featured a percentage and offered a better deal. What might be the text for this ad?

> "Buy 1 get 1 free" is equivalent to 50 percent off each. So, any deal greater than 50 percent is a better deal. For example, the other ad might read, "60 percent off all baseball hats." As a homework assignment, have students find ads and other examples of discounts and use language associated with percentages and ratios to interpret and compare.

11. If you pay 5 percent sales tax on three items, have you paid a total of 15 percent sales tax? Explain your thinking.

> This question will address a misconception that the percent of tax on each item should be added to find the total tax percentage. The distributive property can help students see the flaw in this reasoning. For example, given prices a, b, and c, the total cost—with tax—is $a(0.05) + b(0.05) + c(0.05) = (0.5)(a + b + c)$.

12. Why do stores offer discounts such as 10 percent off when you open a credit card account?

> Since this question requires knowledge of credit card interest, you may wish to pose this question for homework so that students can discuss it with their parents.

130   GOOD QUESTIONS FOR MATH TEACHING

PERCENTAGES (GRADES 7–8)

 13. A local restaurant gives each customer two coupons: One is for 20 percent off the total cost of the meal. The other is for $5 off a purchase of $15 or more. If you have a choice between both coupons, when might the first coupon be the better deal?

> Once students find specific costs that make each coupon the better deal, encourage them to generalize about the cost of any meal if the first coupon is a better deal than the second.

 14. Mekhi used a coupon to buy a new sweatshirt. When he looked at the receipt, he said, "I saved almost $12 using that coupon." What might have been the regular price of the sweatshirt and the deal on the coupon?

> One possible answer: The regular price could have been $47 dollars and the coupon could have read, "25% off."

 15. PT bought a new cage for his pet bird. The total cost was approximately $30 and this included a 5 percent sales tax. What might have been the cost of the cage?

> After students generate a few possible specific answers, encourage them to generalize the form of any possible answer as $a + 0.05(a) \approx 30$ or $1.05a \approx 30$ where a is the cost of the cage. Then, talk about how the generalizations are similar and different.

GOOD QUESTIONS FOR MATH TEACHING   131

CHAPTER 7

GOOD QUESTIONS FOR GEOMETRY

GRADES 5–6	**134**
Two-Dimensional Shapes	*134*
GRADES 7–8	**147**
Two-Dimensional Shapes	*147*
Three-Dimensional Shapes	*153*

The study of geometry invites students to explore, describe, and compare lines, angles, and shapes. When we ask students questions based on these relationships, we are helping them prepare for the more formal study of geometry that will follow in later years.

OVERVIEW

Two-Dimensional Shapes

(Grades 5–6)

Geometry has a language all its own. As students mature mathematically, it becomes increasingly important to use more formal geometric language. Keeping a visible word bank of geometric vocabulary is helpful as we encourage students to refine their talk about geometry.

Experiences at This Level Will Help Students To

- describe, measure, and predict angle measurements formed by intersecting lines with and without a protractor
- explore sums of angle measurements of triangles and quadrilaterals
- classify and compare properties of polygons

Reproducibles are available in a downloadable, printable format. See page xx for directions about how to access them.

Materials

- rulers
- protractors or angle rulers
- blank paper
- ∠HAT (Reproducible 8)
- colored paper
- scissors /glue sticks
- chart paper
- Clock Faces (Reproducible 9)
- Polygon Sets (Reproducible 10)
- Polygon Venn Diagram and Shape Bank (Reproducible 11)
- Polygon Venn Diagram (Extension) (Reproducible 12)
- color tiles
- straightedges
- supply of paper: construction, specialty papers

134   GOOD QUESTIONS FOR MATH TEACHING

OVERVIEW

Good Questions and Teacher Notes (pages 136–146)

> Questions 1 through 3 require the use of a protractor. Protractor usage can be frustrating to upper-elementary-age students. The double scale of the traditional protractor can present difficulties as can figuring out where to put the protractor on the angle! Working through some of the angle vocabulary such as *acute*, *obtuse*, *right*, and *straight* will help students identify reasonable measures. If a student classifies an angle as acute and then finds a measure of 135 degrees, we all know something is amiss! A circle protractor can help with these issues, but practice is once again necessary in order for the students to determine where and how to set the protractor on the angle. The angle ruler that Connected Mathematics Project (CMP) promotes in its lessons is an interesting alternative. Not only can students determine the measurement of an angle, but they can also see how open or closed the angle is by comparing the angle being measured with the angle ruler.
>
> Questions 1 through 3 are based on this model:
>
>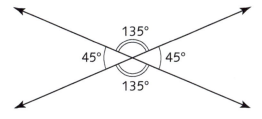

GOOD QUESTIONS FOR MATH TEACHING

GOOD QUESTIONS AND TEACHER NOTES

1. On a blank sheet of paper, construct two intersecting lines. Measure the four angles that the intersecting lines have created. What do you notice about the measures of the angles?

   Construct another pair of intersecting lines. Measure the four angles that these lines have created. What do you notice about the measures of these angles? Can you make a generalization about intersecting lines and the measures of angles that they form?

   > Most students will notice that the *opposite* (*vertical*) angles are equal in measurement. It may be necessary to have students repeat this exercise several times before they can make generalizations.

2. On a blank sheet of paper, construct two intersecting lines. Measure the four angles that the lines have created. What do you notice about the sum of two of the adjacent angles? What about the sum of the other two adjacent angles?

   > Constructions and activities such as this allow students to develop understandings of fundamental geometric theorems. When two lines intersect, two adjacent angles form a straight angle, which measures 180 degrees. This activity can also support a discussion of *supplementary angles*.

TWO-DIMENSIONAL SHAPES (GRADES 5–6)

 3. On a blank sheet of paper, construct two intersecting lines. Measure the four angles that the lines have created. What do you notice about the sum of all four angles? Will this always be the case with any pair of intersecting lines? Why? Support your position with previous investigations [as in Questions 1 and 2] and understandings.

> Questions such as this lay the groundwork for developing the ability to make conjectures, which is integral to the study of formal geometry proof in years to come (Chapin and Johnson 2000, 160).

 4. Given what you know about the measure of a right angle, what is the measure of ∠HAT? Support your position with what you know about angle measurement. If I told you that ∠NAH and ∠HAT were complementary angles, what could you tell me about measures of such angles?

(See Reproducible 8, ∠HAT.)

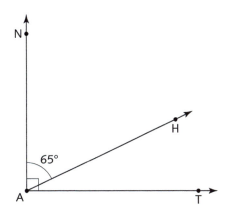

> The study of complementary angles (adjacent angles whose sum equals 90°) gives students another reasoning tool when studying angle measurement.

GOOD QUESTIONS FOR MATH TEACHING   137

GOOD QUESTIONS AND TEACHER NOTES

 5. Without using a protractor, can you determine the measurements of the angles in this construction? Use what you know about vertical angles [they are equal], the sum of adjacent angles [180°], the measurement of right angles [90°], and the sum of the angles that meet at a vertex [360°] to determine angle measures.

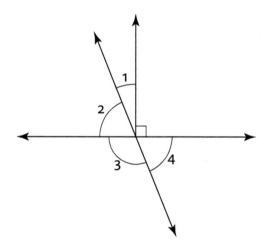

Students may be surprised at what they discover. They quickly make decisions about angle measurements based on what they already know is "true." Students also begin to realize the importance and benefit of reasoning and making conjectures based on informal geometric proof.

138   GOOD QUESTIONS FOR MATH TEACHING

TWO-DIMENSIONAL SHAPES (GRADES 5–6)

 6. On a blank sheet of paper, construct a large triangle using a straightedge. Draw an arc in each angle. Cut out the triangle. Carefully tear off each angle. Reposition the angles so that they touch but do not overlap and glue them down on a piece of colored paper. [See example.] What conjecture can you make about the sum of the angles of a triangle? Will this conjecture apply to all triangles? Try this activity with different triangles.

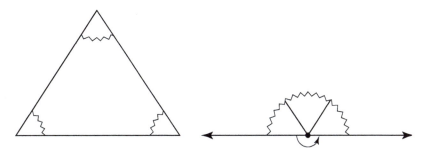

Asking students to make conjectures that are based on self-discoveries and generalizations is necessary when we teach for understanding. Making posters of different triangles and the sums of their angles will tap students' creative energy as well as support their learning.

GOOD QUESTIONS FOR MATH TEACHING

GOOD QUESTIONS AND TEACHER NOTES

7. On a blank sheet of paper, construct a large quadrilateral using a straightedge. Draw an arc in each angle. Cut out the quadrilateral. Carefully tear off each angle. Reposition the angles so that they touch but do not overlap and glue them on a piece of colored paper. [See example.] What conjecture can you make about the sum of the angles of a quadrilateral? Will this conjecture apply to all classifications of quadrilaterals—in particular, regular and nonregular polygons? Try this activity with different quadrilaterals.

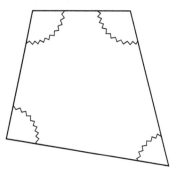
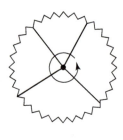

> If following the investigation set up by Question 6, ask students to initially hypothesize about the sum of the measures of the angles of a quadrilateral. Do they think the sum of the angle measures will be greater than that of a triangle's? Or less? Why?

8. Guess My Measure

I am an obtuse angle.

All the digits in my angle measurement are odd.

None of my digits is the same.

The sum of my digits is 13.

All three digits are factors of 9.

The digits are in ascending order.

What is my measure?

Although this may appear to be more of a number riddle than one of geometry, look again! Vocabulary becomes increasingly important as students solve and create geometry riddles. In this particular riddle, understanding the possible range of measures of an obtuse angle (>90° and <180°) is also important.

Having students create their own *Guess My Measure* riddles can help strengthen developing understandings about angle measurement and their use of geometric vocabulary. Creating a class word bank on chart paper of possible vocabulary words that could be used in various riddles can be helpful. Students will also find their knowledge of other mathematical topics helpful when creating clues.

GOOD QUESTIONS AND TEACHER NOTES

9. At 12:00, the hour hand is pointed straight up at the 12. In each clock, mark where the minute hand is at the following times for the other side of an angle. Sketch the angle formed by the hands on the clock and give the measure of the angle without a protractor.

(See Reproducible 9, Clock Faces.)

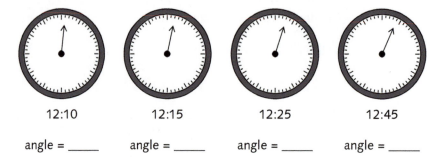

12:10   12:15   12:25   12:45

angle = ____   angle = ____   angle = ____   angle = ____

This activity will help students make the connection between the number of minutes in an hour and the number of degrees in a circle, a measure we adopted from the Babylonians.

Possible follow-up questions: What time creates an obtuse angle? An acute angle? A straight angle? What is so convenient about the number 360 when it comes to degrees?

TWO-DIMENSIONAL SHAPES (GRADES 5–6)

10. How is each polygon the same in each set? Can you find a polygon that does not belong in each set? Can you find another polygon in the same set that might not belong for a different reason?

(See Reproducible 10, Polygon Sets.)

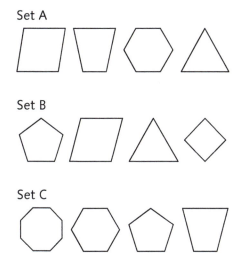

Possible classifications:

SET A: No right angles.

SET B: All are regular polygons.

SET C: All the polygons have at least two obtuse angles.

Questions and investigations that ask students to identify and compare properties of polygons help develop higher levels of geometric thought. Finding properties that classify a set of polygons, as well as counterexamples within a set, can support the development of analytical reasoning skills and informal deductive thought. After completing this investigation, students could be asked to make their own sets and have other classmates determine grouping properties.

GOOD QUESTIONS FOR MATH TEACHING   143

GOOD QUESTIONS AND TEACHER NOTES

> Questions 11 and 12 address similar content but differ in their approach. Questions that present similar content can offer students additional opportunities to make connections between questions and the understandings they have acquired from solving them.

11. Philip has sketched a rectangle. The lengths of the sides of his rectangle add up to 26 inches. What could be the length and the width of Philip's rectangle? Use sketches to support your solution.

Some students may rely on their sketches (the use of color tiles also works well) to determine side length while others may prefer manipulating the numbers. Both methods will demonstrate a working understanding of the properties of rectangles.

12. Is this statement true or false: Any two quadrilaterals that have sides of the same lengths will be identical in size and shape. For example, two quadrilaterals with side lengths of 6 inches, 8 inches, 6 inches, and 8 inches will be the same size and shape. Give explanations and/or sketches to support your thinking.

Although similar to Question 11, this question can also help fine-tune students' abilities to generalize their thinking and develop responses that will, over time, develop into more formal examples of geometric proof.

144   GOOD QUESTIONS FOR MATH TEACHING

TWO-DIMENSIONAL SHAPES (GRADES 5–6)

13. Using the shape bank shown here, place the polygons in the Venn diagram according to their properties.

(See Reproducible 11, Polygon Venn Diagram and Shape Bank.)

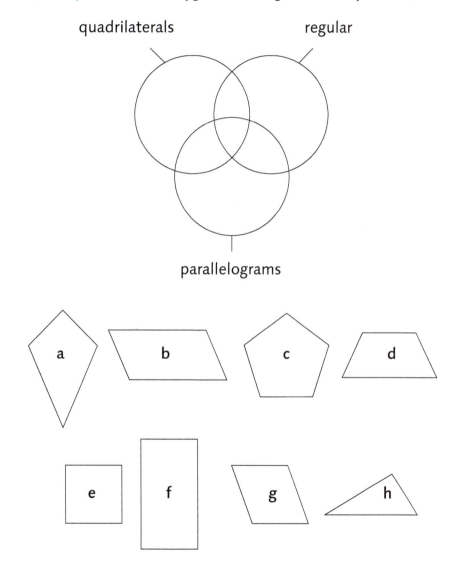

GOOD QUESTIONS FOR MATH TEACHING 145

GOOD QUESTIONS AND TEACHER NOTES

Categorizing polygons according to their properties continues to be important. Understanding that properties can apply to several polygon classifications supports and solidifies the language and meaning of those properties. In order to place a polygon in the Venn diagram, students need to be able to identify the properties as well as apply the language necessary to support their decisions. It extends thinking when a shape is included in the shape bank that adheres to none of the properties—it then lives outside the Venn!

Extend this investigation by offering a Venn diagram populated with the shapes and ask the student to identify the classifications. In this particular Venn, the classifications would be *convex polygons*, *concave polygons*, and *quadrilaterals*. (See Reproducible 12, Polygon Venn Diagram (Extension).)

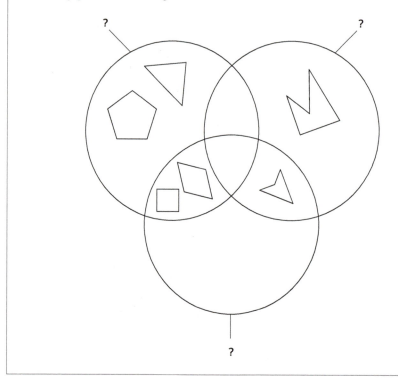

146   GOOD QUESTIONS FOR MATH TEACHING

OVERVIEW

Two-Dimensional Shapes

(Grades 7–8)

Experiences at This Level Will Help Students To

- describe and compare angles that are formed by intersecting lines
- identify lines of symmetry, diagonals, and other characteristics of two-dimensional shapes
- use coordinate graphing to explore dilations, translations, rotations, and reflections of geometric shapes
- determine if figures are congruent or similar
- solve problems about the perimeter and area of two-dimensional shapes
- explore the Pythagorean theorem

Reproducibles are available in a downloadable, printable format. See page xx for directions about how to access them.

Materials

- protractors
- Graph Paper (Reproducible A)
- Rectangle ABCD (Reproducible 13)
- photographs of people in different settings (optional)
- tangrams

Good Questions and Teacher Notes (pages 148–152)

GOOD QUESTIONS FOR MATH TEACHING 147

GOOD QUESTIONS AND TEACHER NOTES

 1. Using your protractor, can you draw three adjacent angles that show at least one acute, one right, one obtuse, and one reflex angle? Name and measure each angle.

One possible answer to this question is shown here.

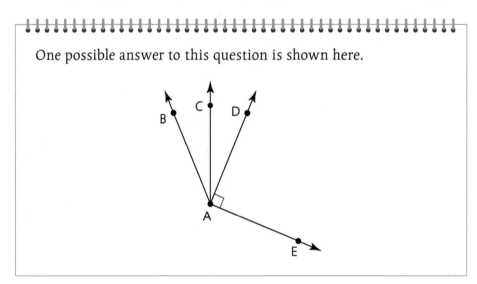

 2. Create a Venn diagram that sorts examples of vertical, adjacent, and linear angles. What do you notice?

By sorting examples of these three types of angles, students will come to realize that all linear angles are adjacent angles and that no adjacent angles are vertical angles.

TWO-DIMENSIONAL SHAPES (GRADES 7–8)

 3. A certain quadrilateral has diagonals that are not lines of symmetry. The quadrilateral has at least one line of symmetry. What might this quadrilateral look like?

> This question helps students focus on the difference between a diagonal and a line of symmetry. This question can be used as a launching pad into a full investigation of the diagonals of quadrilaterals. Classifying quadrilaterals according to their diagonals is a mathematically sophisticated and worthwhile task.

 4. Draw a shape on a piece of graph paper or a coordinate grid whose diagonals have slopes of $\frac{1}{2}$ and -2. (National Council of Teachers of Mathematics 2000)

(See Reproducible A, Graph Paper.)

> The diagonals of each shape will be perpendicular.

 5. We often hear the word *similar* in and out of school. Make a list of all the different situations in which you have heard the word used. How is the use of the word *similar* as used in math class related to its uses outside of math class? (Chapin, O'Connor, and Anderson 2013)

> The various uses of the word *similar* (and many other words in the mathematical register) can cause confusion and lead to misconceptions for students. Discussing how a term varies in usage is crucial to a student's understanding of the concept associated with that term.

GOOD QUESTIONS FOR MATH TEACHING   149

GOOD QUESTIONS AND TEACHER NOTES

6. Describe a series of translations, rotations, and reflections (or slides, flips, and turns) that would move rectangle ABCD from Quadrant II to Quadrant I as shown in the diagram.

(See Reproducible 13, Rectangle ABCD.)

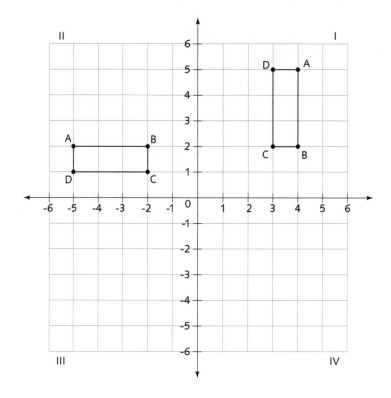

Students should specify the distances of translations, points, and degrees of rotation, as well as orientations of reflections.

TWO-DIMENSIONAL SHAPES (GRADES 7–8)

 7. The coordinates of the vertices of triangle ABC are (2, 1), (4, 1), and (3, 4). Give the coordinates for triangle DEF so that it is similar to triangle ABC. Identify the scale factor from triangle ABC to triangle DEF.

> Students should use graph paper (Reproducible A) to help them think through this question. You can extend this question by asking students to give the coordinates of two new similar triangles.

 8. Police and surveillance companies use similarity to determine the height of suspected criminals caught on videotape. How do they do this? (Lappan et al. 2002)

> Students may need to look at photographs of people surrounded by familiar objects to successfully explore this question.

 9. I sketched a set of seven triangles. Five were similar to one another, three were congruent, and two were neither similar nor congruent to any other. What might these triangles have looked like? Sketch the triangles and label their side lengths.

> This question will help students understand that all congruent shapes are also similar.

GOOD QUESTIONS FOR MATH TEACHING

GOOD QUESTIONS AND TEACHER NOTES

 10. Assigning a value of 1 to the side of the small square in the tangram set, use some pieces to create a figure that has a perimeter that is greater than 6 but less than 7 units.

Students should be comfortable using the Pythagorean theorem to answer this question since the numbers involved are small.

 11. Triangles ABC and DEF are similar but not congruent. The area of triangle DEF is two times the area of triangle ABC. What might be the base and height of each triangle?

Students may make the mistake of doubling both the measures of the base and the height to determine the sides of triangle DEF. Since the area of triangle DEF is twice the area of triangle ABC, each side of DEF is $\sqrt{2}$ times the corresponding length in ABC (e.g., $\frac{1}{2}(3)(4) = 6$ and $\frac{1}{2}(\sqrt{2} \times 3)(\sqrt{2} \times 4) = \frac{1}{2} \times 2 \times 12 = 12$).

 12. Draw a triangle on a coordinate grid whose perimeter is more than 12 units but less than 15 units. Find the perimeter and area of the triangle you create.

You can adapt this question by putting additional constraints on the triangle (e.g., acute and/or isosceles).

GOOD QUESTIONS FOR MATH TEACHING

OVERVIEW

Three-Dimensional Shapes (Grades 7–8)

Experiences at This Level Will Help Students To

- investigate properties of three-dimensional shapes
- create two-dimensional representations of three-dimensional shapes and vice versa
- solve problems about the volume and surface area of three-dimensional shapes

Reproducibles are available in a download-able, print-able format. See page xx for directions about how to access them.

Materials

- Graph Paper (Reproducible A)
- pictures or models of three-dimensional solids including cubes, rectangular prisms, cylinders, cones, and pyramids
- interlocking cubes

Good Questions and Teacher Notes (pages 154–155)

GOOD QUESTIONS FOR MATH TEACHING   153

GOOD QUESTIONS AND TEACHER NOTES

1. Make a case for why each one would not belong to the group:

    cube, rectangular prism, cylinder, cone

> This question helps students see the similarities and differences between three-dimensional shapes. Encourage students to use pictures or models to note similarities and differences between the solids.

2. Describe or draw a three-dimensional shape whose front, side, and top views are different.

> Students may benefit from creating a shape using interlocking cubes before drawing its views.

3. Draw and label the dimensions of a flat pattern for a cylinder. Label the radius of the base and the length and width of the lateral surface.

> Do students understand that the length of the lateral surface must be the same as the circumference of the base?

4. I have a rectangular prism made up of interlocking cubes. Twenty cubes have exactly two faces showing. How many cubes might be in the prism?

> Students will develop their spatial reasoning skills by first answering this question without using the cubes and then checking their answer with the cubes.

THREE-DIMENSIONAL SHAPES (GRADES 7–8)

 5. A large shipping box has twice the volume of a small shipping box. What might be the dimensions, in inches, of each box?

> Students might make the mistake of doubling the dimensions of the smaller box to determine the dimensions of the bigger box. But this would result in a shipping box that had 8 times the volume. One way to answer this question is to double just one dimension of the smaller box. Another is to multiply the dimensions of the smaller box by the cube root of 2.

 6. Cylinder A has twice the volume of Cylinder B but the two cylinders are equal in height. What do you know and what do you wonder about these cylinders?

> Students' answers might include sketches of the cylinders as well as symbolic expressions for the radius of Cylinder A (e.g., if the radius of Cylinder B is r, then the radius of Cylinder A is $\sqrt{2}r$).

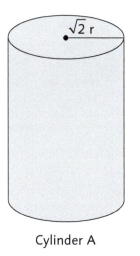

Cylinder A   Cylinder B

GOOD QUESTIONS FOR MATH TEACHING

CHAPTER 8

Good Questions for Algebraic Thinking

GRADES 5–6	**158**
Algebraic Thinking	*158*
GRADES 7–8	**184**
Algebraic Thinking	*184*

lgebra is a vehicle for condensing large amounts of data into efficient mathematical statements (Chapin and Johnson 2000). When we ask students to think algebraically, we are asking them to formalize patterns, analyze change, understand functions, and move fluently between multiple representations of data sets.

157

OVERVIEW

Algebraic Thinking

(Grades 5–6)

The following questions have been created and adapted to develop and support *algebraic thinking* skills, not to promote a formal study of algebra in grades 5 and 6.

Students can be introduced to algebra as a way of thinking in the upper-elementary grades rather than as a formalized unit of study. When we ask students to predict, continue, and articulate patterns, functions, and generalizations, we are asking them to think algebraically. It becomes increasingly important for students to have an understanding of arithmetic procedures as they work to develop algebraic thinking skills. Both are extremely important as students describe mathematical relationships. Whereas arithmetic is effective in describing static pictures of the world, algebraic thinking skills allow students to describe and predict change and variation (Cuevas and Yeatts 2001).

The algebraic principles that these questions address are not necessarily discussed in the commentary following each question. The Lessons for Algebraic Thinking series, published by Math Solutions, is an excellent resource for a discussion of the mathematics being addressed when working with students on algebraic thinking skills. Other resources are cited in the References.

Experiences at This Level Will Help Students To

- understand equality
- understand the use of variables in different situations
- describe function rules using words and symbols
- identify, describe, continue, and generalize patterns
- represent patterns numerically, symbolically, and geometrically

158   GOOD QUESTIONS FOR MATH TEACHING

OVERVIEW

Reproducibles are available in a download-able, print-able format. See page xx for directions about how to access them.

MATERIALS

- Number Path A (Reproducible 14)
- Number Path B (Reproducible 15)
- color tiles
- Graph Paper (Reproducible A)
- Patio Borders (Reproducible 16)
- Pencil Sharpener Stories and Graphs (Reproducible 17)
- As Time Goes By Graphs (Reproducible 18)
- Grouping Patterns (Reproducible 19)

GOOD QUESTIONS AND TEACHER NOTES (PAGES 160–183)

GOOD QUESTIONS FOR MATH TEACHING   159

GOOD QUESTIONS AND TEACHER NOTES

 1. In the following equations, the same shapes are the same numbers.

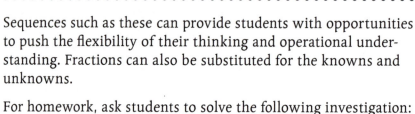

What number does each symbol represent?

> Sequences such as these can provide students with opportunities to push the flexibility of their thinking and operational understanding. Fractions can also be substituted for the knowns and unknowns.
>
> For homework, ask students to solve the following investigation:
>
> Given the same values listed above for □, △, and ⌂, what is the value of ◇? [(3 × □) + (2 × △)] − ◇ = 2 × ⌂

 2. Find values for *a* and *b* that would make this number sentence true.

$168 + a = b$

If $a = 12$, what is the value of *b*?

If the value of *a* increases, how will the value of *b* change? If the value of *a* decreases, what happens to the value of *b*?

> When we ask students to identify and generalize relationships, we are asking them to think algebraically. Many standard substitution questions can be extended to encourage students to identify patterns and operational relationships.

ALGEBRAIC THINKING (GRADES 5–6)

3. $\square + 0 = \square$ is a true sentence no matter what number is substituted for $\square$. Can you find other open number sentences that are true no matter what value is substituted for the unknown? Test your sentences by substituting values for the unknown(s).

> Questions such as this ask students to contemplate the existence of *identities*—open sentences that become true equations no matter what value is substituted for the unknown.
>
> Students may claim that $\square \div 0 = \square$. Take time to discuss why division by zero is not possible. It is not possible to "undo" or reverse this equation: $\square \times 0 \neq \square$. Posting an ongoing list of found identities can be helpful for students as they discover mathematical properties such as the commutative property: $\square + \triangle = \triangle + \square$.

4. Match the "If" and "then" statements to make true sentences. Prove your selections.

If $n = 7$,   a. then $n^2 = 49$

If $n = 12$,   b. then $(2n + 3) \div 4 = 5$

If $n = 0$,   c. then $24 - (n + 6) = 6$

If $n = 8.5$, d. then $(12 - n) \times \frac{1}{2} = 6$

> Computational practice is embedded in the solving and creation of "If . . . then" statements such as these. Other values of n and subsequent equations can be developed based on the computational skills being covered in class at the time.

GOOD QUESTIONS FOR MATH TEACHING

GOOD QUESTIONS AND TEACHER NOTES

5. What numbers can *a*, *b*, and *c* stand for? Can you find other solutions? What is always true about *c*? Why? What is always true about *b*? Why?

$$\begin{array}{r} a \\ + a \\ \hline cb \end{array}$$

Trial-and-error calculation will allow students the opportunity to generalize truths about the values of *a*, *b*, and *c*. Because there are multiple solutions, truths can be compared and contrasted in a class discussion.

6. Can all of these statements be true? Explain why or why not. Can you insert another relational symbol to make this progression of statements true? Support your solutions with numerical proof.

A > B

B > C

C > D

D > A

Algebra has a language of its own. Terminology should be used when the question presents a meaningful context for its usage. Understanding the difference between a *relational symbol* (one that designates a relationship between two quantities) and an *operational symbol* (one that designates an action, such as +, −, ×, or ÷) becomes increasingly important as students move toward more formal algebra instruction. Experimenting with other symbols and the substitution of numerical values will give students valuable thinking and articulation practice.

ALGEBRAIC THINKING (GRADES 5–6)

 7. What is the start number? Justify your solution.
(See Reproducible 14, Number Path A.)

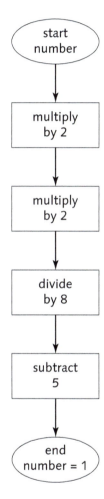

Undoing operations sets the stage for later work with simplifying equations. Have students create their own number paths, making sure that they work both forward and backward.

GOOD QUESTIONS FOR MATH TEACHING   163

GOOD QUESTIONS AND TEACHER NOTES

8. What is the end number when the start number is 5? What is the start number when the end number is 16? What is the start number when the end number is 40?

What do you know about the start number when you know the end number?

What do you know about the end number when you know the start number?

(See Reproducible 15, Number Path B.)

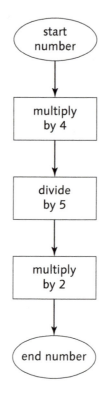

Looking for relationships between numbers and operations can help students predict and generalize patterns and/or outcome. Have students explore the following question for homework: Choosing a start number that is a multiple of 5 will result in an end number that is a multiple of 8. Why do you think that happens?

164 GOOD QUESTIONS FOR MATH TEACHING

ALGEBRAIC THINKING (GRADES 5–6)

9. Complete the chart. What is the rule? Write your rule in words and as an equation. Add three more pairs of In and Out values.

In	Out
5	8
10	13
3	6
0	?
?	45
?	?
?	?
?	?

Asking students to identify relationships between the In column and the Out column is asking them to identify functions. For every In value, there is only one Out value, which is linked by a specific rule.

Often students will prefer to look for progressions *vertically*. Encourage students to also look *horizontally*. Not giving In values in numerical order pushes students to look at horizontal patterns.

Although the rule given in this particular chart may appear to be simple for some (+3), it presents a starting point that is accessible to all students. More complex rules can then be introduced as students become more comfortable and competent. When students make up their own sets of In and Out values, they seem to create increasingly complex rules naturally!

For homework, ask students to create a set of In and Out values for a classmate to solve.

GOOD QUESTIONS FOR MATH TEACHING

GOOD QUESTIONS AND TEACHER NOTES

 10. Complete the chart. What is the rule? Add three more pairs of In and Out values.

In	Out
aardvark	a
giraffe	a
hippo	o
?	?
?	?
?	?

Even when using words, the Out value relies on a rule that links it to the In value. Starting with *aardvark* purposefully confuses students because the Out value for this particular set is the *second* vowel of the In value. Students begin to realize that it is often necessary to study several In and Out pairs before they can generalize a rule.

Assign the following question for homework: Create a set of In and Out values *not* based on numerical values. You can use pictures, words, or designs. Be able to articulate your rule clearly.

 11. Complete the chart. What is the rule? What would be the output value for any value (n)?

In	1	2	3	4	5	10	n
Out	4.5	7.5	10.5	13.5	?	?	?

Presenting another charting representation other than the traditional vertical T-chart can be helpful for students as they develop flexibility in their thinking. Asking students to create a set of In and Out values for a classmate to solve for homework can be a continued meaningful application of this question.

GOOD QUESTIONS FOR MATH TEACHING

ALGEBRAIC THINKING (GRADES 5–6)

 12. Read the following. At this rate, how many finches will arrive at the feeder on the tenth day? Create a chart to identify the pattern. Explain the pattern in words.

My bird feeder is set up for winter.

On the first day, five finches come to my feeder.

On the second day, six finches come to the same feeder.

On the third day, seven finches arrive.

Each day, the number of finches increases by one more than the number of finches that arrived at the feeder the day before.

> The ability to create tables and/or T-charts (horizontally and vertically) to chart and extend patterns is a useful problem-solving tool. The ability to then articulate and symbolically represent those patterns is equally useful. Use the following question as a homework assignment:
>
> > *On the first day, five finches come to my feeder. If the number of finches increases by four each day, how many finches will arrive at the feeder on the tenth day?*
>
> Create another T-chart to continue the pattern. Explain the pattern in words.

GOOD QUESTIONS FOR MATH TEACHING   167

GOOD QUESTIONS AND TEACHER NOTES

 13. What would come next in this sequence?

1, 4, 9, __, __, __

Can you draw a picture to represent this growth? Can you write a rule in words and symbols to find the next term? Can you find another way to represent the growth of this pattern?

> Because this pattern represents exponential growth, a question such as this could accompany a number theory unit. Each term can be represented by a square formation, which can help students identify the squareness of the numbers.
>
> This sequence can also be represented graphically, which can help students see the nonlinear, non-constant growth of the sequence. For homework, ask students to follow the same procedure for this sequence: 1, 3, 6, __, __, __, __.

ALGEBRAIC THINKING (GRADES 5–6)

 14. Using color tiles, create a pattern of squares that fits this T-chart describing its growth.

Stage Number	Total of Squares
1	3
2	6
3	9
4	12
5	15

How is your pattern growing? Sketch your pattern. Describe your rule in words. Compare your pattern with a classmate's.

What is the same about your patterns and growth? What is different?

How many squares would there be in the tenth stage? How do you know? In the one hundredth?

How many tiles would be in any stage (nth stage)?

You should encourage students to describe predictable growth. When growth is predictable, students can see it by looking at what stays the same at each stage *and* at what changes.

The *Piles of Tiles* activity from *Lessons for Algebraic Thinking, Grades 3–5* (Wickett, Kharas, and Burns 2002, 197) presents various investigations such as this in greater detail and depth.

GOOD QUESTIONS FOR MATH TEACHING

GOOD QUESTIONS AND TEACHER NOTES

 15. Imagine that the following pattern continues:

Row 1	3				
Row 2	3	6			
Row 3	3	6	9		
Row 4	3	6	9	12	
Row 5	3	6	9	12	15

What numbers will be in Row 6?

What is the last number in Row 10?

In which row is 45 the last number?

Explain how to find the last number in a row.

Looking at the row numbers and the last numbers in each row can help students identify the pattern.

Row Number	1	2	3	4	any row
Last Number	3	6	9	12	row number × 3

Note that the In and Out (*x* and *y*) values in Questions 14 and 15 are representations of the same growth pattern.

170 GOOD QUESTIONS FOR MATH TEACHING

ALGEBRAIC THINKING (GRADES 5–6)

 16. The students in Mr. Variable's math class were playing *Guess My Rule*. Mr. Variable presented pairs of starting and final values and the students were asked to use the information to determine the rule. Mr. Variable wrote the first pair in the extended T-chart as shown here (Lawrence and Hennessy 2002).

Starting Value	Using the Rule	Final Value
4		12

What could the rule be? Do you know for sure? Why or why not?

Once students realize that one pair of values is not enough information to determine a function rule, ask them to name two additional pairs of values and a rule that works for all three pairs. There may be multiple rules for which these two values could apply!

GOOD QUESTIONS AND TEACHER NOTES

 17. During another round of *Guess My Rule*, the students in Mr. Variable's class correctly identified the rule as "The final value is three less than twice the starting value." What three pairs of starting and final values could be placed in this table that would satisfy this rule? (Lawrence and Hennessey 2002)

Starting Value	Using the Rule	Final Value
	Final Value = 3 less than twice the starting number	

> Ask this question once students have had many experiences determining the rule when given the starting and final values. See *Lessons for Algebraic Thinking, Grades 6–8* (Lawrence and Hennessey 2002) for more information about *Guess My Rule* protocols and applications. You may wish to use the discussion of this question to introduce some important terms and relationships in the study of functions. For example, you could explain to students that the starting values can also be called the *domain* of the function and the final values can be called the *range* of the function.

ALGEBRAIC THINKING (GRADES 5–6)

 18. The pattern continues. Fill in the blanks.

2 × 4 + 1 = 3 × 3

3 × 5 + 1 = 4 × 4

4 × 6 + 1 = __ × __

__ × 7 + 1 = __ × __

__ × __ + __ = __ × __

Describe patterns that you see.

What will the equation look like when the first term is 25?

Asking students to identify and continue patterns within patterns helps develop their abilities to continue multiple patterns within a sequence. Equality is also addressed in problems such as these because of the need to operate on both sides of the equation.

GOOD QUESTIONS FOR MATH TEACHING   173

GOOD QUESTIONS AND TEACHER NOTES

19. Look at the pattern in the figures that follow. If the pattern continues, how many white squares will be in the border of a patio with one hundred shaded squares? Explain how you know. Can you give a rule to determine how many squares will be in this border?

(See Reproducible 16, Patio Borders.)

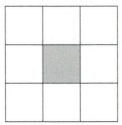

Patio 1: 1 shaded
8 white

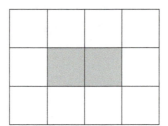

Patio 2: 2 shaded
10 white

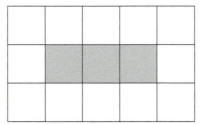

Patio 3: 3 shaded
12 white

174 GOOD QUESTIONS FOR MATH TEACHING

ALGEBRAIC THINKING (GRADES 5–6)

Thinking algebraically requires students not only to determine what comes next in a pattern but also to generalize beyond a geometric representation. A multicolumned T-chart can be used to organize the data for this problem. Asking students to look at patterns both vertically and horizontally will help them generalize patterns and make predictions.

Patio Number	Number of Shaded Tiles	Number of Border (White) Tiles	Total Number of Tiles in Patio
1	1	8	9
2	2	10	12
.	.	.	.
.	.	.	.
.	.	.	.

GOOD QUESTIONS FOR MATH TEACHING   175

GOOD QUESTIONS AND TEACHER NOTES

 20. Which graph matches which story?

(See Reproducible 17, Pencil Sharpener Stories and Graphs.)

You are working on a math investigation and you realize that your pencil needs to be sharpened . . .

| Story A | You get up. Walk toward the pencil sharpener. Stop to answer a question at Molly's table. Walk on to the pencil sharpener. Sharpen your pencil. Walk back to your table. | Story B | You get up. Walk to the pencil sharpener. Sharpen your pencil. Walk back. On the way back, you drop your pencil and break its point. Stop and laugh with Avel. Pick up pencil. Walk back to the pencil sharpener to resharpen the pencil. |

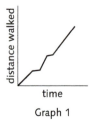

Graph 1

Graph 2

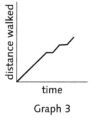

Graph 3

Graphic and symbolic representations of motion are common in the formal study of algebra. In answering this question, students are asked to compare *intervals of time* with *intervals of distance walked* as they fit stories to graphs. A conversation about the inappropriateness of Graph 2 for either story given its shape may be necessary.

176 GOOD QUESTIONS FOR MATH TEACHING

ALGEBRAIC THINKING (GRADES 5–6)

 21. This graph represents Lindsay's time and distance during a 10K run. How would you describe the course?

A graphic representation is a story about relationships between two values within a given context. If you give students one and ask them to create the other, you are offering students opportunities to construct understandings about such relationships.

GOOD QUESTIONS FOR MATH TEACHING   177

GOOD QUESTIONS AND TEACHER NOTES

 22. Without graphing the points, determine which graph fits these ordered pairs. How can you tell?

(2, 3)   (2, 6)   (2, 4.5)   (2, 0)

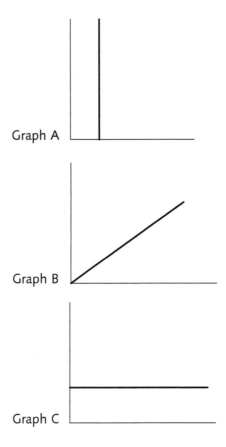

> Asking students to assess and make generalizations about graphs as they identify change and constant values can support them as they learn to reason about graphic representations and relationships. Ask students to answer the following for homework: Explain graphs in which the *y* values are the same. What could the graph look like? Create a situation or story in which these values would make sense.

ALGEBRAIC THINKING (GRADES 5–6)

23. What could be happening in these graphs? What could be changing (or not) as time goes by? Choose a graph and create a story that describes the change.

(See Reproducible 18, As Time Goes By Graphs.)

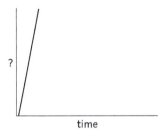

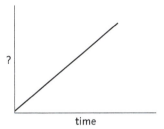

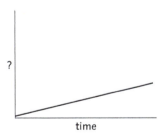

Looking at graph shapes without numbers on either axis allows students opportunities to make conjectures about the qualities of the shape of each graph, such as the steepness of the line (*slope*) and growth or change over time.

GOOD QUESTIONS FOR MATH TEACHING   179

GOOD QUESTIONS AND TEACHER NOTES

24. Write a number sentence that fits the picture of the groupings here. Are there other ways you can group the dots? Write a number model for each new grouping.

(See Reproducible 19, Grouping Patterns.)

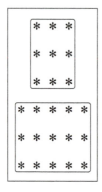  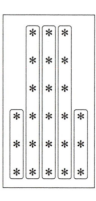 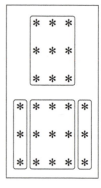

Responses:

15 + 9 = 24   3(3) + 3(5) = 24   2(3) + 3(6) = 24   2(9) + 2(3) = 24

Because each picture has a total of twenty-four dots, equality can be demonstrated by comparing two number models, such as 15 + 9 = 2(3) + 3(6). It becomes increasingly important to challenge a common misconception that equates the equals sign with *the answer is* rather than a representation of balance and equivalence. If creating number models to fit the picture is difficult for some students, ask them to match the number models to the pictures.

Engaging children's literature can offer meaningful contexts within which to explore patterns and functions. Questions 25 and 26 follow an oral reading of *The Five-Dog Night* (Christelow 1993). A more detailed write-up of The *Five-Dog Night* explorations can be referenced in *Enriching Your Math Curriculum, Grade 5: A Month-to-Month Resource* (Schuster 2010).

ALGEBRAIC THINKING (GRADES 5–6)

 25. Construct a three-column T-chart to represent the "dog night" and the number of feet in Ezra's bed. As you work, notice the x- and y-values and how they grow and change.

x Dog Night	What Is Happening?	y Number of Feet in the Bed
1	2 + 4	6
2	2 + 4 + 4	10
3	2 + 4 + 4 + 4	14
4		
5		
10		
100		
Any dog night		

What about a warm night — when there are no dogs needed in the bed? What would that look like in the T-chart?

How is the pattern growing? Why is there always a 2 in the What Is Happening column? What does that term represent? Why does that make sense?

What is the rule for this pattern?

- Describe the rule in words.
- Now describe the rule in symbols: $y = ?$

Students will want to connect the coldness of the night to the number of dogs in the bed but may need some support and guidance through discussion as they work to articulate the functional relationship (rule) found in the story. Students may very well focus on the number of feet on the dogs in the bed—but forget about Ezra! The visual image of Ezra in the bed is not only entertaining, it greatly supports the concept of a *constant* in an equation.

GOOD QUESTIONS FOR MATH TEACHING

GOOD QUESTIONS AND TEACHER NOTES

 26. Using the T-chart from the previous question, construct a coordinate graph to represent the pattern of feet in Ezra's bed as the nights get colder.

What will the *x*-axis be labeled? Why does that make sense?

What will the *y*-axis be labeled? Why does that make sense?

Where is Ezra (the constant) in the graph?

Identify the terms of the equation of the growth of this pattern in the graph:

- Where do you see the 2?
- Where is the 4?
- Where is the *x*?
- Where is the *y*?

This graph represents a *linear function*. Why does that explanation make sense?

ALGEBRAIC THINKING (GRADES 5–6)

The story of the growth of the number of feet in the bed has been told in the previous two questions: in a T-chart, in words, in a rule, in a graph, and it can also be told in pictures. The growth is *constant* and *predictable*; hence, a representation of a *linear function*. A drawing of the pattern growth can be added to the five representations of this growth story. It is important and powerful for fifth and sixth graders to understand how all these representations tell the same story.

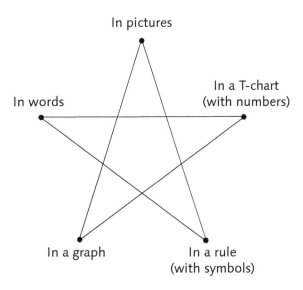

Telling the story . . .

- In pictures
- In words
- In a T-chart (with numbers)
- In a graph
- In a rule (with symbols)

A meaningful extension of this question could be: Identify and create the five representations of the growth pattern in the story *Minnie's Diner* (Dodds 2004). Compare and contrast the growth pattern of *The Five-Dog Night* and *Minnie's Diner*. How are they the same? How are they different? Which growth pattern represents a *linear function*? Which a *nonlinear function*? Why do those descriptions make sense?

OVERVIEW

ALGEBRAIC THINKING
(GRADES 7–8)

EXPERIENCES AT THIS LEVEL WILL HELP STUDENTS TO

- identify proportional and linear relationships
- compare properties of linear and proportional relationships across representations (e.g., tables, graphs, and equations)
- express pattern rules both iteratively and explicitly
- understand a function as a relationship between an input and an output variable such that for each input there is exactly one output
- use variables to represent quantities in real-world and mathematical problems
- use properties of operations to generate equivalent expressions
- identify the rate of change and initial value of a linear relationship
- solve linear equations in one variable
- connect systems of two linear equations to their related graphs

Reproducibles are available in a downloadable, printable format. See page xx for directions about how to access them.

MATERIALS

- Graph Paper (Reproducible A)
- Walk-a-Thon Graphs (Reproducible 20)
- Perimeter and Area Tables (Reproducible 21)

GOOD QUESTIONS AND TEACHER NOTES (PAGES 185–198)

184   GOOD QUESTIONS FOR MATH TEACHING

ALGEBRAIC THINKING (GRADES 7–8)

1. Write an equation for a line that is less steep than the line shown.

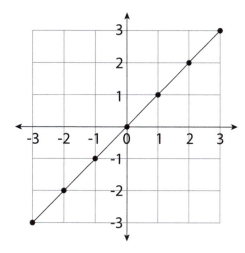

Developing a visual benchmark for $y = x$ and comparing it with other linear equations are important parts of developing algebraic reasoning.

2. JR looked at a table of values for a linear relationship between two variables, x and y. JR said, "I can tell right away that the relationship between x and y is not proportional." Sketch a graph and create a table of (x, y) coordinate pairs that meet this description.

This question targets the relationship between proportional and linear relationships. Even though every proportional relationship is linear, not every linear relationship is proportional.

GOOD QUESTIONS FOR MATH TEACHING

GOOD QUESTIONS AND TEACHER NOTES

3. For two variables, *x* and *y*, each time *y* changes by 1, *x* changes by 3. The relationship between *x* and *y* is linear but not proportional. Create a table of values (*x*, *y*) that satisfies this description.

> You may also ask students to create a graph and equation for the relationship modeled by their tables.

4. Nadia and Raphael plan to take part in a dance-a-thon. They will ask sponsors to donate money for each hour that they dance. They each made a chart that showed the relationship between money raised per sponsor and hours danced. Nadia and Raphael looked at their charts and made the following statements:

Nadia: The amount of money I will raise will be ten more than my time.

Raphael: The amount of money I will raise will be twice as much as my time.

What do these statements reveal about how Nadia and Raphael will earn their donations?

> Students may benefit from making charts that show the changes in the amount of money raised for Nadia and Raphael in order to answer this question.

ALGEBRAIC THINKING (GRADES 7-8)

 5. Two walkers in a walk-a-thon graphed their distance over time. They looked at their graphs and noticed that their lines were parallel. What does this reveal about the walkers? If they had made tables comparing distance to time, how would their tables be similar? How would they be different?

(See Reproducible 20, Walk-a-Thon Graphs.)

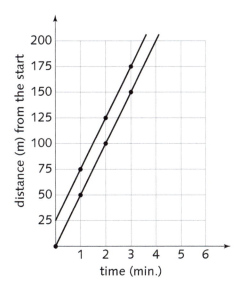

Since parallel lines have the same slope, the walkers have the same walking rates but different starting points. To help students understand this, ask them to make a chart of distance over time for each walker and compare and contrast the data.

GOOD QUESTIONS FOR MATH TEACHING   187

GOOD QUESTIONS AND TEACHER NOTES

6. Imani was studying for an upcoming math test. She looked back at her notes from a class on patterns made from pattern blocks. She found the following two statements:

   Each stage has a constant of four blocks plus one block for each stage number.

   Each stage has one more block than the previous stage.

   She wondered if it was possible that these two generalizations were describing the same pattern. What do you think? How do you know?

   > It is possible that the generalizations describe the same pattern since the first is an explicit rule and the second is an iterative rule. One way for students to develop proficiency with explicit rules is to connect them with iterative rules for the same pattern.

7. Jair and Hermine were making growth patterns using square tiles in math class. They looked at one pattern and made the following statements:

   Jair: I see a constant of two and then add the stage number.

   Hermine: I see a constant of one and then add one more than the stage number.

   Is it possible that Jair and Hermine were looking at the same pattern?

   Why or why not?

   > Describing explicit rules for patterns is often a challenge for students in the middle grades. This challenge is further complicated by the fact that there are often many ways to describe a rule explicitly (Lawrence and Hennessy 2002). Talking in math class about how explicit rules for the same pattern are alike can help students with this challenge.

ALGEBRAIC THINKING (GRADES 7–8)

8. Find words that complete the following sentences.

   a. The _____ of a square is a function of its _____.
   b. The _____ of a circle is a function of its _____.
   c. There is a functional relationship between _____ and _____.
   d. _____ is not a function of _____.

   > This question provides an opportunity to discuss a function as a relationship between variables such that for each input there is exactly one output. You may also want to classify each relationship as linear or nonlinear.

9. What is the same and what is different about how the letter M has been used in the following statements?

   Aiden jumped 3 m.

   $3 \times m = m \times 3$ for all numbers m.

   If $3m + 2 = 14$, then $m = 4$.

   > Because letters have so many different uses in mathematics, it is important not only to present students with mathematical statements that use letters in various ways but also to specifically discuss what role the letter plays in each situation.

GOOD QUESTIONS FOR MATH TEACHING   189

GOOD QUESTIONS AND TEACHER NOTES

 10. Vicker looked at the set of ordered pairs in the following table and said, "There is not a functional relationship between *x* and *y* because there are two inputs for one output." Do you agree or disagree with Vicker's statement? Explain.

x	y
-10	100
-5	25
-3	9
0	0
3	9
6	36
10	100

This question highlights a common misconception about functions that for each output there is exactly one input. The set of ordered pairs does show a functional relationship since each input is paired with exactly one output.

 11. The following sign is posted at the Clarence Library:

FINE POLICY FOR OVERDUE BOOKS

Twenty-five cents per day plus an additional $0.50 for reshelving. Maximum fine of $5.

Create a table or graph for the library to display to help people calculate their fines.

Have students post their tables and graphs. Then explore the relationships between the words, the chart, and the graph. For example, ask students how to use an entry in the chart to find a point on the graph and vice versa. Ask students how to use the wording of the policy to locate a specific point on the graph and vice versa.

ALGEBRAIC THINKING (GRADES 7–8)

 12. Sabina earns money by babysitting. She offers her clients two different payment options and presents them in the graph shown here. What might each payment option be? (National Council of Teachers of Mathematics 2000)

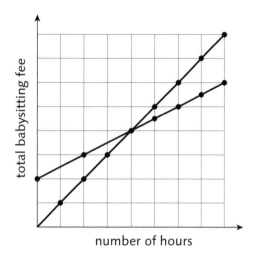

Once students explain what they think the options are, ask them why parents would choose either payment plan. The context of this question can be changed to other situations such as checking account balances, parking lot rates, and distance traveled over time.

13. Mario is investigating a problem about growing squares. The side length of the squares grows from 1 to 2 to 3 units, and so on. The perimeters and areas of the squares change accordingly. Mario made a chart to show the relationship between the side length and the perimeter and another to show the relationship between the side length and the area. If Mario were to make a graph of each set of data, how would the graphs be similar? How would they be different?

(See Reproducible 21, Perimeter and Area Tables.)

Side Length	Perimeter
1	4
2	8
3	12
10	40

Side Length	Area
1	1
2	4
3	9
10	100

Focus the discussion of this question on rates of change. Students should observe that both charts show growth, but one shows growth at a constant rate while the other does not. Spend time discussing how this difference in rate of change will affect the look of the graphs.

ALGEBRAIC THINKING (GRADES 7–8)

 14. Hamdi and Julie have two different cell phone plans. They want to compare them to see if one offers a better buy. They each made a graph showing the relationship between the number of calls and the total money owed. They made the following statements:

Hamdi: My graph has a greater rate of change than yours.

Julie: My graph has a greater initial value than yours.

What do these statements reveal about Hamdi's and Julie's cell phone plans? What might a sketch of their graphs look like?

> Exploring their applications in real-life contexts gives meaning to the concepts of *rate of change* and *initial value*. Extend this question by asking if the line showing Hamdi's data will ever cross the line showing Julie's data and what this means about determining which plan offers the better buy.

 15. Jean Pierre's teacher asked him to identify the rate of change for the linear equation $y = 3x + 4$. Jean Pierre thinks there must be some mistake since 3 is a whole number and not a ratio. How might you respond to Jean Pierre?

> A whole number m expresses the associated unit rate (i.e., change in rise per unit change in run) for the ratio of rise to run. In the given equation, the rate of change is 3:1, which is represented by the coefficient of x in the linear term $3x$.
>
> Extend this question by asking these two questions, which push for generalizations about slope: When is m a whole number? When is m a fraction?

GOOD QUESTIONS FOR MATH TEACHING

GOOD QUESTIONS AND TEACHER NOTES

16. Carla and Fiona are having a mathematical debate about the equation $y = \frac{1}{2}x + 3$. Carla thinks that every time y changes by 1, x changes by 2. Fiona thinks that every time y changes by $\frac{1}{2}$, x changes by 1. What do you think?

> Students should use multiple representations to support their positions including graphing the equations and making a table of values. They may also decide to use what they know about equivalent and complex fractions to support their positions.

17. For homework last night, Jorge had to simplify four expressions. He wrote his answers without copying the original expressions. What might they have been?

   a. $10x + 3$

   b. $-\frac{1}{2}$

   c. $12x$

   d. $-3x - 6$

> This question focuses on combining like terms. Look for the following common mistakes in students' answers:
>
>   a. $10x + 3 = 10 + x + 3$
>   b. $-\frac{1}{2}x = -\frac{1}{2} + x$
>   c. $12x = 12 + x$ or $(4x)(3x)$
>   d. $-3x - 6 = -3(x - 2)$

194   GOOD QUESTIONS FOR MATH TEACHING

ALGEBRAIC THINKING (GRADES 7–8)

 18. Write three other expressions that are equivalent to the expression $6 - 4(x + 1)$.

> Be on the lookout for the mistake that $6 - 4(x + 1)$ is equivalent to $2(x + 1)$.

 19. Jojo used the equation $2(x + 4) = 20$ to solve a problem about a two-dimensional shape. What might the problem have read?

> Be sure that students connect the meaning of the variable in the equation to the context of their problem. For example, the problem could be: *The perimeter of a rectangle is 20 units. The width is 4 units. What is the length?* In the given equation, x represents the length of the rectangle.

 20. Explain how the two equations below are similar and different.

$$y = \tfrac{2}{3}x + 5 \qquad 1 = \tfrac{2}{3}x + 5$$

> As students begin to formulate and discuss their answers, ask follow-up questions as needed so that students see the connections between the two linear equations. For example, students might note that the equation on the right corresponds to the point $(x, 1)$ on the line modeled by the equation on the left.

GOOD QUESTIONS FOR MATH TEACHING

GOOD QUESTIONS AND TEACHER NOTES

  21. What might be the linear equation for the line sketched here?

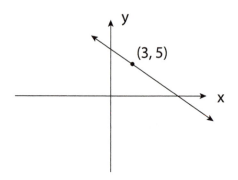

Although infinitely many answers are possible, all equations should have a negative value for the slope and positive value for the y-intercept and contain the point (3, 5).

  22. Copy and complete the table shown so that the (x, y) coordinate pairs represent points on one line.

x	y
-10	
-8	
-3	
0	
2	
11	

Tables with x values that do not change in predictable or orderly ways encourages students to think about rate of change in terms of equivalent ratios.

ALGEBRAIC THINKING (GRADES 7–8)

 23. **Write a linear equation for a line that passes through quadrants II, III, and IV only.**

You may need to review the notation system for the four-quadrant coordinate grid before assigning this question. By convention, the quadrants are labeled with roman numerals I, II, III, and IV starting in the upper right quadrant and going around counterclockwise. If students answer this question by graphing a line on graph paper (Reproducible A), share several possible answers and discuss what they all have in common. For example, all lines that pass through only quadrants II, III, and IV, have a negative y-intercept and negative slope (e.g., $y = -3x - 4$).

 24. **Write a two-step linear equation where the solution is $x = -\frac{4}{3}$.**

If students struggle to answer this question, you might ask, "If $x = -\frac{4}{3}$ is the final step in the solution process, what might have been the step that came immediately before?"

GOOD QUESTIONS FOR MATH TEACHING   197

GOOD QUESTIONS AND TEACHER NOTES

  25. A system of two linear equations is sketched here. What might be the two equations in the system?

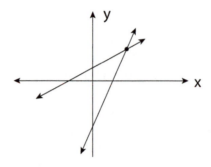

Although infinitely many answers are possible, both equations should have a positive rate of change (slope) but only one should have a positive *y*-intercept. You can extend this question by providing a value for the point of intersection of the two lines and asking students to derive two possible equations for the system.

  26. Some of the numbers in the system of linear equations shown have been erased. Find possible values that create a system with no solutions.

$$y = \frac{?}{31}x - ?$$
$$y = \frac{7}{?}x - 91$$

The equations featured in the system feature "unfriendly" numbers as a way to encourage students to use rate of change and initial value—instead of algebraic manipulation—to find their answers. You can extend this question by asking students to find possible values that create a system with either exactly one solution or infinitely many solutions.

CHAPTER 9

Good Questions for Data Analysis and Probability

GRADES 5–6	**200**
Data Analysis	*200*
Probability	*208*
GRADES 7–8	**216**
Data Analysis	*216*
Probability	*223*

In middle school, students are asked not only to collect and display data but also to discuss, analyze, and understand the correspondence among data sets and their graphic representations (National Council of Teachers of Mathematics 2000). Questions that ask students to reflect on notions of chance will help them better understand and apply basic concepts of probability to their daily lives.

GOOD QUESTIONS AND TEACHER NOTES

DATA ANALYSIS (GRADES 5–6)

EXPERIENCES AT THIS LEVEL WILL HELP STUDENTS TO

- develop strategies for collecting, representing, comparing, and reporting data
- analyze data sets according to statistical landmarks such as *mean*, *median*, *mode*, *range*, and *sample size*

Reproducibles are available in a downloadable, printable format. See page xx for directions about how to access them.

MATERIALS

- chart paper
- Graph Paper (Reproducible A)
- Mystery Line Plots (Reproducible 22)
- Investment Graphs (Reproducible 23)

GOOD QUESTIONS AND TEACHER NOTES (PAGES 201–207)

200   GOOD QUESTIONS FOR MATH TEACHING

DATA ANALYSIS (GRADES 5–6)

> Some of the following questions require making charts and/or graphs that will represent data about a particular class. It will be necessary to post chart paper with directions about the particular data collection before students answer the questions.

1. On a large sheet of chart paper, make a Venn diagram with two circles. Label the circles "I Love Fractions" and "I Love Mystery Novels" or any other classifications that you think would be interesting to your students. Have students place their names in the Venn where they belong, reminding students to place their names on the outside of the Venn if they fit neither category.

   What does it mean if someone is placed outside the two circles? What does it mean if someone is placed in the intersection? Write three statements about your classmates from the data displayed on the Venn diagram.

   > As students grow in mathematical maturity and sophistication, it becomes equally important for them to be able to express their opinions and observations with greater clarity. Posing a simple question such as, "What do you notice?" offers opportunities for students to refine their wording and written conclusions.

2. The sixth grade is planning a movie night in the theater. Ziva is conducting a survey about movie interests of the sixth graders in order to gather information for possible movie choices. If Ziva asks her classmates one categorical question and one numerical question, what could the questions be?

   > A question such as this asks students to think about the *kinds of responses* a data set can generate, not necessarily the data set itself.

GOOD QUESTIONS FOR MATH TEACHING   201

GOOD QUESTIONS AND TEACHER NOTES

3. Post the following question on the board or on a piece of chart paper:

   What is your favorite field game (e.g., soccer, baseball, SPUD, etc.)?

   Have this data available for students as they answer the following questions.

   Organize this data into a line plot. What is the mode of the data?

   Who would be interested in this data?

   What would the data tell them?

   Does your data have a mean? Why or why not?

   > Students can be easily confused as they try to articulate the difference(s) between numerical and categorical data. Although this data can be graphed and analyzed, it is *categorical*, which makes finding a mean impossible.

4. Make a data set representing the ages of students with the following statistical landmarks:

   Sample size: 12 students

   Range: 8 years

   Median age: 12.5 years

   Mode: 10 years

   Will everyone's data set look the same? Why or why not?

   > Creating their own data sets requires students to have greater understanding of the identified statistical landmarks. Working backward, as students are being asked to do in this question, can be difficult for some. Sharing possible data sets as a class will help those who find this type of thinking difficult.

DATA ANALYSIS (GRADES 5–6)

 5. The mean number of children in six families is four. How many children might be in each family? Can you make a line plot to represent this data?

> Some students may approach this as a factors-and-multiples problem. Others may create a line plot first and adjust the data as they fit the plot to the constraints of the problem. The approach students take in answering this question may prove to be more enlightening than the answers they come up with.

 6. Atul and Lauren have just bought a pet rabbit. The owner of the pet store told them that the median life span of a rabbit is seven years. What could a data set for the life span of twenty-five rabbits look like?

> Given the information in the question, students may assume that *every* rabbit will have a median age of seven, *every* rabbit will live to be only fourteen years old, and/or the highest piece of data *must* be fourteen. Discussions about outliers, sample size, and even the general health of those rabbits in the data set can set up convincing arguments in support of any of the positions. A question such as this can also lead students to the realization that data does not always help us make informed choices.

GOOD QUESTIONS AND TEACHER NOTES

 7. Each plot on this chart shows a different set of data about a sixth-grade class. Match the plots with the given data sets and justify your choices (Everyday Learning Corporation 2002).

(See Reproducible 22, Mystery Line Plots.)

```
                              X
                        X  X  X
                        X  X  X  X        X        X
            X           X  X  X  X  X  X  X     X        X
   X                    X  X  X  X  X  X  X     X        X        X
  ─────────────────────────────────────────────────────────────────
  52 53 54 55 56 57 58 59 60 61 62 63 64 65 66 67 68 69 70 71
```
Plot 1

```
                                          X
                     X       X  X         X     X
  X        X         X       X  X         X     X        X  X  X
 ─────────────────────────────────────────────────────────────────
  48 50 52 54 56 58 60 62 64 66 68 70 72 74 76 78 80 82
```
Plot 2

```
        X
  X     X
  X     X     X
  X     X     X
  X     X     X     X        X        X        X
 ─────────────────────────────────────────────────
  0     1     2     3        4        5        6
```
Plot 3

```
                              X
                        X  X      X     X
            X     X     X  X  X   X     X        X
  ──────────────────────────────────────────────────
  26 28 30 32 34 36 38 40 42 44 46 48 50 52 54
```
Plot 4

```
                          X
           X              X              X     X
  X        X     X        X     X        X     X              X
 ─────────────────────────────────────────────────────────────
  0   1    2     3        4     5    6   7     8     9        10
```
Plot 5

204   GOOD QUESTIONS FOR MATH TEACHING

DATA ANALYSIS (GRADES 5–6)

Data Sets   **Plot Number**

A. Number of hours watched of TV last night   _____

B. Ages of younger brothers and sisters   _____

C. Heights, in inches, of some sixth graders   _____

D. Ages of some sixth graders' grandmothers   _____

Explain how you selected the line plot for Data Set D.

Explain why you think the other line plots are not correct for Data Set D. What data set could represent Plot 4? Explain your thinking.

What other answers did you consider for each set of data? How did you exclude data sets for each line plot?

Identifying what is likely versus what is unlikely will help students match the data sets with the line plots. The range and distribution of the data will help students make judgments and conclusions.

GOOD QUESTIONS FOR MATH TEACHING   205

GOOD QUESTIONS AND TEACHER NOTES

 8. Mrs. Jacobs gave a math unit test worth 100 points. Following the test, she organized the scores into a stem-and-leaf plot.

State five conclusions Mrs. Jacobs could make about her students' performance. Make reference to vocabulary words such as *range*, *median*, *mean*, *mode*, and *sample size* in your conclusions.

What do you think the unit of study was? Why?

Tens	Ones
5	1 6 8
6	3 5 5 6 8
7	3 6 6 6 7
8	2 5 6
9	0 2

Stem-and-leaf plots offer students opportunities to identify clusters and patterns in a data set rather than focus on individual data items. Stem-and-leaf plots are also helpful when data covers a large range. Giving students opportunities to discuss and apply chosen representations of numerical data (e.g., line plot, bar graph, stem-and-leaf plot) will help them better assess appropriate and useful representations.

DATA ANALYSIS (GRADES 5–6)

 9. Which of these two graphs would you choose to convince potential consumers to invest in your company? Why? (Chapin and Johnson 2000).

(See Reproducible 23, Investment Graphs.)

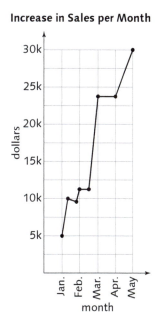

Both graphs display the same data. Because the intervals on the x- and y-axes are different on the two graphs, one *appears* to show more rapid growth. Graphs can be deceiving and improperly scaled to prove to consumers what producers want to prove!

GOOD QUESTIONS FOR MATH TEACHING 207

OVERVIEW

PROBABILITY (GRADES 5–6)

The study of probability can cut across all strands of mathematics. The applied arithmetic required by probability activities is rich and varied. Probability questions can and should accompany many units of study. Introduce a day of probability study as a diversion from the everyday occurrences of math class, designating it as "Probability Monday" or whichever day it is.

EXPERIENCES AT THIS LEVEL WILL HELP STUDENTS TO

- understand that some events involve chance
- understand the concepts of likely and unlikely, fair and not fair
- develop strategies for reporting and interpreting both experimental and theoretical probability
- understand that probabilities are useful for making decisions

Reproducibles are available in a downloadable, printable format. See page xx for directions about how to access them.

MATERIALS

- Dart Board (Reproducible 24)
- Bags of Marbles (Reproducible 25)
- Blank Spinner Faces (Reproducible C)
- colored pencils
- marbles (red, blue, and yellow)
- color tiles
- crayons
- linking cubes

GOOD QUESTIONS AND TEACHER NOTES (PAGES 209–215)

208   GOOD QUESTIONS FOR MATH TEACHING

PROBABILITY (GRADES 5–6)

1. The probability of a particular event happening is $\frac{2}{5}$. Explain the probability of the event not happening. What could the event be?

> A number line can be a helpful visual aid to support students' thinking about the relative certainty of an event happening.
>
> | | 50% | |
> | --- | --- | --- |
> | | $\frac{1}{2}$ | |
> | 0 | | 1 |
> | impossible   less likely   more likely   certain |
>
> Asking students to identify the probability of an event *not* happening can be counterintuitive. As we help students develop probabilistic thinking skills, we need to offer them opportunities to identify and/or differentiate between events that will *always* happen, those that will *sometimes* happen, and those that will *never* happen.

GOOD QUESTIONS FOR MATH TEACHING

GOOD QUESTIONS AND TEACHER NOTES

 2. Assign Regions A, B, C, and D to this dartboard on which the probability of landing on Region A is $\frac{5}{8}$.

If Courtney threw sixty-three darts, how many might land in Region A? Explain your reasoning.

How can your understanding of fractions help you with this task?

(See Reproducible 24, Dart Board.)

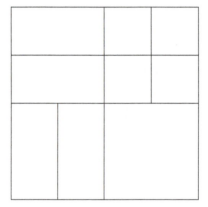

Although students may intuitively realize that they are manipulating fractional parts when answering this question, we need to offer students opportunities to explicitly make those connections between concepts and procedures.

PROBABILITY (GRADES 5–6)

3. To play this game at a math carnival, a player picks one marble from each bag. Bag 1 contains equal amounts of red, blue, and yellow marbles. Bag 2 contains equal amounts of red and blue marbles. If the colors of the marbles match, the player wins a prize.

(See Reproducible 25, Bags of Marbles.)

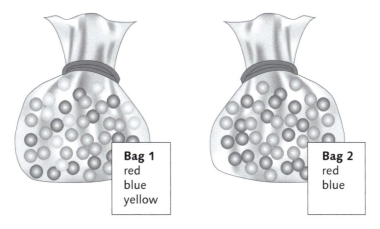

What are the possible outcomes of the game?

What are the chances that a player will win a prize?

Is this a fair game? If not, how could you change the rules or the game so that it would be a fair game? Explain your thinking. What are the possible outcomes of your new game in support of your adjustment(s)?

> Charting outcomes is a valuable mathematical tool. Tree diagrams, matrices, and pictures can all be useful representations.
>
> It's important to determine the purpose of this question before you pose it. Will this question be used as an opportunity to teach charting techniques? Or can you assume that students have a level of proficiency with techniques of charting, which will then allow them to focus on the fairness of the game?

GOOD QUESTIONS FOR MATH TEACHING

GOOD QUESTIONS AND TEACHER NOTES

 4. Describe how you could make a spinner that had four equally likely outcomes. What fraction of the circle would each section be?

Make a drawing of your spinner using colored pencils. Can you think of another way to divide the spinner? Make a drawing of that spinner as well.

(See Reproducible C, Blank Spinner Faces.)

> Students may quickly divide the spinner into four equal adjacent parts. Asking them to come up with another way to divide the spinner will give students the opportunity to apply what they already know about fractions. Dividing up a spinner into eight equal regions with two each of the same color—but not adjacent to each other—may generate some interest. If time allows, have students test out their different arrangements.

 5. Design a spinner with five spaces so that the chance of landing in one space is twice the chance of landing in each of the other four spaces. Give the degree measurements of each central angle.

(See Reproducible C, Blank Spinner Faces.)

> Probability questions such as this not only assess an understanding of how likely an event is to happen but also offer students opportunities to practice computational skills.

PROBABILITY (GRADES 5–6)

6. Suppose that out of one hundred spins, you land on red eighty-two times and you land on blue eighteen times. What might your spinner look like? Color in your spinner. Explain your reasoning. How confident are you in your decision?

(See Reproducible C, Blank Spinner Faces.)

> Some students may color 82 percent of the spinner red and 18 percent blue whereas some may color 75 percent red and 25 percent blue, saying that not enough spins were made to determine exact percentages. The more spins, the closer the spins will come to the actual percentages or the theoretical probability of the action.
>
> Assign the following questions for homework: Suppose out of 300 spins, you land on red 222 times and land on blue 78 times. What does your spinner look like now? How does this spinner differ from your last spinner? How confident are you in your decision now?

7. Sarah has designed a spinner with red, blue, yellow, and green sections. The chance of landing on red is 50 percent, the chance of landing on blue is 30 percent, and the chance of landing on yellow or green is 10 percent each. Suppose you spun Sarah's spinner 50 times. How many times would you expect to spin red? Blue? Yellow? Green? What if you spun it 100 times? How about 150 times? Explain your thinking.

> It is helpful to let students make conjectures and to support those conjectures with an understanding of probable outcomes. Look for thinking that demonstrates an understanding that spinning more times can move the experimental probability closer to the theoretical. Asking about possible outcomes after 225 spins will stretch those students who are ready for a challenge.

GOOD QUESTIONS FOR MATH TEACHING   213

GOOD QUESTIONS AND TEACHER NOTES

 8. Imagine that you have three colors of marbles in a bag: red, yellow, and blue.

Imagine that you could pick out one marble without looking.

The probability of picking a red marble is $\frac{1}{2}$.

The probability of picking a yellow marble is $\frac{1}{3}$.

And the probability of picking a blue marble is $\frac{1}{6}$.

How many marbles of each color could be in the bag? How do you know? What could a picture of your answer look like?

There are many possible entry points when answering this question. Some students may actually want to try the experiment. Having bags and red, yellow, and blue marbles available (or color tiles, linking cubes, or crayons) may be necessary for some students. Drawings may help. Some students may move straight to paper-and-pencil calculations and the use of common denominators:

$$\frac{1}{2} + \frac{1}{3} + \frac{1}{6} = 1$$
$$\frac{3}{6} + \frac{2}{6} + \frac{1}{6} = 1$$

At the very least, there would be three red marbles, two yellow marbles, and one blue marble.

As an extension, pose a similar question with different fractions of marbles that add up to 1. For example: There are four different colors of marbles in a bag: red, green, yellow, and blue. The probability of pulling out a red or a blue marble is $\frac{1}{4}$. The probability of pulling out a green marble is $\frac{1}{3}$. The probability of pulling out a yellow marble is $\frac{1}{6}$. What is the fewest number of marbles of each color that could be in the bag? How do you know?

214 GOOD QUESTIONS FOR MATH TEACHING

PROBABILITY (GRADES 5–6)

9. Coco has a spinner that is divided into four regions. She spins the spinner multiple times and records the results in the following table:

Region	1	2	3	4
Number of times spinner lands in that region	7	12	3	26

Based on the table, make a drawing of what the spinner would look like. Why does your drawing make sense?

A question such as this is open to many variations based on specific mathematical objectives. The number of regions can be adjusted as well as the counts.

10. Baseball player Speedy Sanchez has tried to steal second base thirty-two times so far this season. He has been successful twenty times. Do you think his chances of stealing second base the next time he tries are good or bad? Explain your reasoning. Can you base your decision solely on the numbers, or could there be other circumstances that might affect Speedy's percentage of stolen bases?

Making assumptions based on approximations can be useful. Knowing that Speedy steals successfully more than 50 percent of the time is often enough to start a conversation about his success rate.

Interesting conversations may be initiated by your baseball aficionados that may be based on opinions about the significance of the pitcher or an infielder. In this case, the numbers may not tell the whole story when it comes to statistics, probability . . . and baseball!

GOOD QUESTIONS FOR MATH TEACHING

OVERVIEW

Data Analysis (Grades 7–8)

Experiences at This Level Will Help Students To

- write questions, design studies, and gather data about a characteristic of a population
- use data taken about a sample to make conclusions about the population from which the sample was taken
- choose, create, and apply appropriate graphical representations of data sets including histograms, stem-and-leaf plots, box-and-whisker plots, and scatter plots
- interpret and compare data using measures of center and measures of variability
- use scatter plots for bivariate measurement data to investigate patterns of association between two quantities

Materials

- optional: calculators

Good Questions and Teacher Notes (pages 217–222)

DATA ANALYSIS (GRADES 7–8)

1. Imagine you wanted to find out the favorite movie of students in your school. How would you accomplish this? What are the advantages and disadvantages to your plan?

> This question presents a good opportunity to discuss different types of sampling, such as random sampling, convenience sampling, and voluntary response sampling.

2. A local newspaper reporter wrote an article claiming that more than 75 percent of the town's citizens thought the library fines were too high. Many readers wrote to the editor refuting the report, claiming that the sample for the survey was biased. How might the sample have been biased?

> Helping students develop the ability to look beyond the headlines and evaluate their validity is an important skill in today's data-driven world.

3. You read in an ad:

   Four hundred more people prefer the new and improved Bright Smile toothpaste to another brand.

   How might this data be misleading? (Lappan et al. 2002)

> Students should consider the size of the sample as well as the way the survey was conducted (e.g., to what other toothpaste was the new and improved Bright Smile compared?) when answering this question.

GOOD QUESTIONS FOR MATH TEACHING

GOOD QUESTIONS AND TEACHER NOTES

 4. In a recent survey, 0.685 of people surveyed said they participate in voluntary recycling. Write an attention-grabbing headline about this statement.

> Share a variety of answers so that students can see how various forms of rational numbers can be used to report statistics. For example, "Almost 70 percent of survey respondents participate in voluntary recycling." As an extension, ask students to find headlines that contain quantitative statements about a data set.

 5. Ayumi asked twenty-five of her classmates, "How many hours a night do you spend on homework?" She organized all of the responses into the box-and-whisker plot shown here. Write three conclusions about the data set.

> A box-and-whisker plot marks the minimum value (excluding outliers), lower quartile (median of the data below the median), the median, the upper quartile (the median of the data above the median), and the maximum value (excluding outliers). Students should answer this question after they have had experiences interpreting and constructing box-and-whisker plots.

DATA ANALYSIS (GRADES 7–8)

  6. Recently, two members of the student council surveyed the seventh-grade class and organized the data in the box-and-whisker plot shown here. What might their survey question have been?

Once students determine a sensible survey question, ask them to interpret the results using what they know about box-and-whisker plots. For example, a student might think that the survey question was "How many pets do you own?" That student should then be able to say, "Approximately half of those surveyed own two or more pets."

  7. The double box-and-whisker plot shown here was created using data from a school survey. What do you notice and what do you wonder about the plot and the data sets?

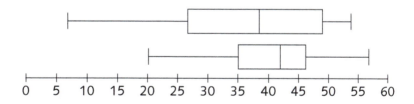

Be sure that students' answers address the variability of the data as represented by the "box" or middle 50 percent of each data set.

GOOD QUESTIONS FOR MATH TEACHING

GOOD QUESTIONS AND TEACHER NOTES

8. Ian's ice-cream shop opens at 11:00 a.m. and closes at 7:00 p.m. One day, Ian kept track of the number of customers in his shop each hour (on the hour) and recorded the information in a histogram. He noticed that the range of customers was 20, and, on average, the number of customers in the store each hour was 12. What might the histogram look like?

> Note whether students construct the histogram correctly. Since each bar in a histogram represents an interval, the bars should be drawn without spaces separating them. Students will need to decide which measure of center to consider for the average.

9. KJ was interested in the relationship between arm span and height. She recorded the arm span and height of each member of her class and made a double stem-and-leaf plot to show her data. KJ said, "There is a cluster of six people who are 'squares'—they have the same arm span as height." Do you agree with this statement?

Height in Inches		Arm Span in Inches
999887776	5	366677778888999
5332211110000	6	0000112

> Students should realize that KJ's conclusion is faulty since the double stem-and-leaf plot separated the arm length and height for each person. A good follow-up question could ask students to consider graphs that *would* help KJ look for relationships between height and arm span.

DATA ANALYSIS (GRADES 7–8)

 10. In Mrs. Marvel's class, a student's grade is determined by the average of their seven test scores each term. At a recent parent-teacher-student conference, the following exchange occurred:

Mrs. Marvel: Tim's average is a C. And I have the data to show it.

Tim: I have an A average. And I have proof.

Tim's parents: Looking at your test scores, it looks to us like your average is a B.

How could all three have proof of three different grades?

> This question focuses on the discrepancies between the three measures of central tendency (mean, median, and mode). Spend time having students share data sets of seven test scores that show the three different averages.

 11. A recent survey asked a group of students to rate, on a scale of 1 to 3, how much they enjoyed the school lunches. The mean (average) rating was 1.8 and the mean absolute deviation was 0.7. What conclusions might you make about students' enjoyment of school lunch?

> One of the most prevalent real-life applications of decimals is data reporting. So it is important for students to learn how to interpret data reported with decimals.

GOOD QUESTIONS FOR MATH TEACHING   221

GOOD QUESTIONS AND TEACHER NOTES

 12. VJ was interested in how his classmates spend their time on the weekend. He wrote a statistical question, created a survey, collected the data, and made the scatter plot shown here. Unfortunately, he forgot to label the axes. What might be the two measurement variables for VJ's data set?

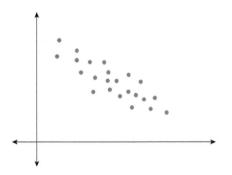

One way to answer this question is to note that the scatter plot shows a strong negative correlation between the two variables. Then students can think of two variables related to VJ's topic that have this kind of relationship. For example, the *x*-variable might be screen time and the *y*-variable might be time spent playing sports.

 13. A scatter plot was used to model the relationship between two measurement variables; the equation $y = 0.75x + 10$ was a good fit for the data set. Sketch a scatter plot that meets this description. Name at least three data points that might be in the data set.

Watch for students who only consider points where the value of *y* is exactly equal to $0.75x + 10$. Students need to understand that a line that "fits" the data is a good fit for approximating the overall pattern and may not hit many (or any) of the points.

222   GOOD QUESTIONS FOR MATH TEACHING

OVERVIEW

PROBABILITY (Grades 7–8)

EXPERIENCES AT THIS LEVEL WILL HELP STUDENTS TO

- use tree diagrams, area models, organized lists, and knowledge of fractions to reason about chance
- find and analyze probabilities of compound events
- calculate probabilities of events when drawing with and without replacement
- use experimental probabilities to reason about theoretical probabilities and vice versa
- find the expected value of an outcome

Reproducibles are available in a downloadable, printable format. See page xx for directions about how to access them.

MATERIALS

- calculators
- dice of two different colors
- number tiles
- color tiles
- Blank Spinner Faces (Reproducible C)

GOOD QUESTIONS AND TEACHER NOTES (PAGES 224–230)

GOOD QUESTIONS FOR MATH TEACHING   223

GOOD QUESTIONS AND TEACHER NOTES

1. A cafeteria serves a lunch each day that consists of one appetizer, one main course, and one dessert. The selections are made randomly from a limited number of items that does not change all year. Chinua figured out that the probability of getting her favorite meal (carrot sticks, tuna fish on rye, and chocolate pudding) was $\frac{1}{24}$. How many appetizers, main course, and desserts might the cafeteria choose from each day?

> While some students may be able to answer this question using the fundamental counting principle, others may need to make a sample menu.

2. Ryan thinks that the chance of rolling a sum of 4 with two dice is the same as rolling a sum of 5 because he thinks there are two ways to roll a 4 [(1, 3) and (2, 2)] and two ways to roll a 5 [(1, 4) and (2, 3)]. Do you agree or disagree? Why?

> There are actually four ways to roll a sum of five, (1, 4), (4, 1), (2, 3), and (3, 2), and three ways to roll a sum of four, (1, 3), (3, 1), and (2, 2). Students often think that rolling (1, 4) is the same as rolling (4, 1) and count these two possible ways as one way. In the discussion of this question, have two different colors of dice available to help students make the distinction between different ways to reach a particular outcome.

PROBABILITY (GRADES 7–8)

3. Thiago wants to play a game at a carnival where he'll open one of several boxes. Inside one of these boxes are some envelopes. Inside one of these envelopes is a hundred-dollar bill. Thiago figured out correctly that he has a $\frac{1}{12}$ chance of winning. How many boxes and how many envelopes might there be?

> Encourage students to use an organizational tool, such as a tree diagram or an area model, to answer this question.

4. Maddie is playing a board game in which she rolls two dice, adds the numbers rolled, and moves that number of spaces on the board. Maddie can win the game on her next move if she rolls any one of three sums. She figures out that her probability of winning is $\frac{1}{4}$. What sums do you think Maddie needs to roll?

> Ask this question only after students have analyzed the likelihood of all possible outcomes of rolling two dice.

5. Jamie's favorite radio station is hosting a contest. At 8:00 a.m. tomorrow, the first fifteen callers will qualify for a chance to win a free trip to Hawaii. Only one of the fifteen callers will win the trip and the winner will be chosen randomly. Jamie figures she has a $\frac{1}{15}$ chance of winning the trip. Do you agree? Why or why not?

> Jamie needs to first consider the probability of being one of the first fifteen callers, which could be quite slim. Her chance of winning the trip is *dependent* on her chance of being one of the fifteen callers.

GOOD QUESTIONS FOR MATH TEACHING

GOOD QUESTIONS AND TEACHER NOTES

6. A bag is filled with number tiles marked 1 or 2. If you reach into the bag twice, with replacement, it is very unlikely to pull out two tiles marked 1.

How many number tiles marked 1 and 2 might be in the bag?

What might be the total number of tiles?

> Once students answer this question, you may wish to extend it by asking what the probability would be if the tiles were drawn without replacement.

7. Tessa pulled color tiles from a bag and found that the experimental probability of drawing two red tiles without replacement was 35 percent.

How many red tiles might have been in the bag?

What might the total number of tiles have been?

> Since the given probability is experimental, a variety of answers is possible. For example, there may have been four red tiles and six tiles total, which would result in a 40 percent chance ($\frac{4}{6} \times \frac{3}{5} = \frac{12}{30} = 40\%$) of picking red, without replacement, which is close to 35 percent.

PROBABILITY (GRADES 7–8)

8. A weather reporter predicts that there is approximately a 40 percent chance of having rain on both days of the weekend. What might be the chance of rain each day?

> Weather reports rely heavily on probability. Therefore, instruction on probability should help students make sense of what they hear and read in these reports. One way to answer this question is to use an area model.
>
>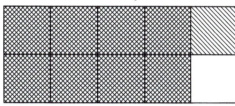

9. Austin was playing a game with a spinner. He figured out that if he spun the spinner one hundred times, about thirty-eight of the spins would land on the region(s) marked with an A. What might this spinner have looked like?

(See Reproducible C, Blank Spinner Faces.)

> This question requires students to create a representation that matches a given probability. One way to answer this question is to recognize that $\frac{38}{100}$ is close to $\frac{37.5}{100}$ which is equal to $\frac{3}{8}$. So approximately $\frac{3}{8}$ of the spinner should be marked with an A.

GOOD QUESTIONS FOR MATH TEACHING

GOOD QUESTIONS AND TEACHER NOTES

 10. A spinner is divided into red, blue, and green sections. Jafari expects that for every three spins that land on red, two will land on blue, and there will be approximately three times as many red spins as green. What might this spinner look like?

(See Reproducible C, Blank Spinner Faces.)

> Help students connect the comparative language in this question with the probabilities of spinning each color by constructing representations. For example, since there will be three times as many red spins as green, the probability of spinning red must be three times the probability of spinning green.

 11. Ruby spun a spinner that was divided into different-colored sections. After spinning thirty times, she wrote the following in her notebook.

"P(not blue) ≈ 40%."

What might this spinner look like?

(See Reproducible C, Blank Spinner Faces.)

> Use this question to motivate a discussion about the relationship between experimental and theoretical probabilities.

PROBABILITY (GRADES 7–8)

 12. The makers of Marla's favorite candy bar are having a contest. There is a coupon for a free candy bar hidden inside some candy bars. The candy bars cost $0.60 each. Marla reads the probability of winning on the package and figures out that she would probably need to spend about $10.00 in order to win a free candy bar. What do you think is the chance of winning a free candy bar?

> After sharing students' answers to this question, discuss whether or not this is a fair contest.

 13. Leah and Sam were playing a game with two dice. They took turns rolling the dice and finding the products of the numbers rolled. To make the game fair, if Leah rolls a certain product she gets 2 points. If Sam rolls a certain product, he gets 3 points. What might the products be?

> The inverse relationship between probability and payoff points is challenging for many students. For example, the probability of rolling Leah's product must be 1.5 times *greater* than that of rolling Sam's number since Leah gets 1.5 times *fewer* points than Sam.

GOOD QUESTIONS FOR MATH TEACHING

GOOD QUESTIONS AND TEACHER NOTES

 14. Jorge was thinking about playing a game at his town fair. He calculated his probability of winning the $5 prize and found that if he plays ten times, he can expect a profit of $10.

How much might the game cost to play?

What might be the probability of winning this game?

> One possibility is a cost of $1 and a four-in-ten chance of winning: Jorge would spend $10 playing the game and win four times for a profit of $10.

CHAPTER 10

GOOD QUESTIONS FOR MEASUREMENT

GRADES 5–6	**232**
Temperature, Time, and Length	*232*
Weight	*235*
Area and Perimeter	*240*
Volume	*250*
GRADES 7–8	**257**
Weight	*257*
Area	*261*
Length and Perimeter	*265*
Volume and Capacity	*271*

In order to help students understand measurement, it is important to ask questions that will require them to both measure and make connections between the many relationships within measurement systems. Many measurement questions can be asked in conjunction with the study of other mathematical strands. We can use measurement to explore geometry, to collect and analyze data, and to develop proportional reasoning skills. The base ten conversions inherent to the metric system can also lend themselves well to the study of place value and decimal fractions. In the United States, the task of choosing appropriate measurement units is complicated by the use of both the customary and the metric systems of measurement. Whenever possible, students should be given the opportunity to develop familiarity with both systems.

OVERVIEW

Temperature, Time, and Length (Grades 5–6)

Experiences at This Level Will Help Students To

- understand the importance of standard units
- estimate, make, and use measurements
- compute with and convert within customary units of measure

Reproducibles are available in a downloadable, printable format. See page xx for directions about how to access them.

Materials

- chart paper
- Graph Paper (Reproducible A)

Good Questions and Teacher Notes (pages 232–234)

1. On March 4 at 10 a.m., the temperature in Boston was 33°F. The temperature rose and fell throughout the day. At 5 p.m., the temperature had fallen to 27°F. What might the temperature have been at each hour?

> Interpreting the positive or negative change on a thermometer can help students identify changes in temperature as well as give them a vertical number line reference.

232 GOOD QUESTIONS FOR MATH TEACHING

TEMPERATURE, TIME, AND LENGTH (GRADES 5–6)

 2. **Fill in the blanks with numbers. Make sure that the numbers apply to the context of the story!**

It was a beautiful June day. The temperature was _____°C at 7:30 a.m. Two and a half hours later, at _____, the temperature was _____ degrees warmer, or _____°C. Three and a half hours later, at _____, the temperature had risen to 30°C.

> A variety of procedures can be used to answer this question, such as guess-and-check or working backward from 30°C. The sense made by the chosen numbers is what matters most.

 3. **[Ask students to post their bedtimes and waking times for school days and nights on chart paper as they come into class. Then ask the following questions.]**

What is the range of sleep hours?

What is the median number of hours of sleep for our class on a school night? What is the mean number of hours? What is the mode?

What is the typical number of hours of sleep that your classmates are getting a night? Is this more or less than you thought it would be?

> Asking students to define what is typical for a data set pushes them to analyze and categorize data. Some may focus on the mode. Some may focus on the median. Some may focus on the distribution of data.

GOOD QUESTIONS FOR MATH TEACHING   233

GOOD QUESTIONS AND TEACHER NOTES

4. I am a measure of time.

    You can measure the length of a math class with me.

    There are sixty of me in an hour.

    I am equal to sixty seconds.

    Guess my unit.

> Asking students to devise their own *Guess My Unit* riddles with four or five clues will support students as they make connections between units of measure and identify attributes of their chosen measures.

5. What is your arm span in millimeters? centimeters? meters?

    If you find one measurement, how can you find the others without measuring?

> Greater understanding (and appreciation!) of the ease of metric conversions between units will develop when students are asked to measure with different units as well as to calculate one unit from another.

6. Five students measured the length of an animal footprint. The average measurement was between 8 and 9 inches. What might each measurement be?

> Students might choose median or mean for the measure of average. Be sure to also discuss why there are different measures for the same length.

234   GOOD QUESTIONS FOR MATH TEACHING

OVERVIEW

WEIGHT (GRADES 5–6)

EXPERIENCES AT THIS LEVEL WILL HELP STUDENTS TO

- understand the importance of standard units
- estimate, make, and use measurements
- compute and compare weight measurements and conversions

Reproducibles are available in a downloadable, printable format. See page xx for directions about how to access them.

MATERIALS

- drawing paper and supplies (markers, colored pencils, crayons)
- Weights (Reproducible 26)
- dry rice and beans
- measuring cups
- scale

GOOD QUESTIONS AND TEACHER NOTES (PAGES 236–239)

GOOD QUESTIONS FOR MATH TEACHING   235

GOOD QUESTIONS AND TEACHER NOTES

1. Make lists or pictures of things that weigh:

   a. less than 1 kilogram

   b. between 1 kilogram and 5 kilograms

   c. between 5 kilograms and 20 kilograms

   d. between 20 kilograms and 50 kilograms

   e. more than 50 kilograms

> Personal references or benchmarks can help make the process of estimation more accessible for students. U.S. customary measurements can easily be substituted.

2. Are these claims reasonable? Justify your position.

   a. My math teacher weighs 2,400 ounces.

   b. My math teacher drinks 70 ounces of water a day.

> Both claims are reasonable. If an adult weighs 150 pounds, they should drink 50 percent of their body weight *in ounces*, according to many weight and conditioning coaches. Questions such as this give students the opportunity to develop a meaning for *ounce* given a context of weight or volume.

WEIGHT (GRADES 5–6)

3. You want 5 pounds of weights. You have the following weights. Choose the fewest number of weights that totals 5 pounds. List the weights and numbers of each. Keep a record of your thinking.

(See Reproducible 26, Weights.)

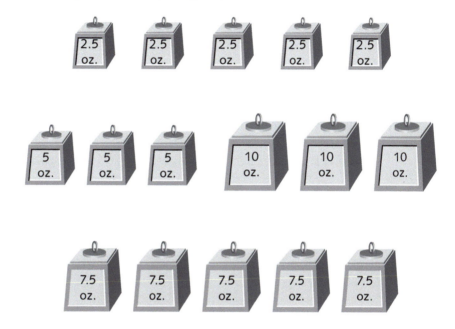

Students are given the opportunity to practice calculation as well as conversion skills.

GOOD QUESTIONS FOR MATH TEACHING

GOOD QUESTIONS AND TEACHER NOTES

4. Rufus Mayflower, the toothpaste millionaire (Merrill 1999), knows that 500 pounds is a quarter of a ton. Decide which of the following equations best represents how Rufus could have determined this. How do you know?

   a. $2{,}000 \times 4 = n$

   b. $2{,}000 \div n = 25$

   c. $2{,}000 \div 4 = n$

   d. $2{,}000 \times n = 4$

   Why did Rufus use the number 2,000? Why did he use the number 4? Could Rufus have figured out how many pounds are in a quarter of a ton any other way?

   > Problem-solving strategies are employed when choosing the best representation. Asking students to explain why the other representations are not appropriate can be helpful when processing answers. Other quantities can be used to create similar questions, such as cups and gallons or ounces and pounds.

5. Many cooks around the world consider this expression to be a reasonable estimate:

   A pint's a pound the world around.

   What does this expression mean?

   > One pint equals 2 cups. The rule implies that 1 cup of a food item weighs about $\frac{1}{2}$ pound, or 8 ounces.

WEIGHT (GRADES 5–6)

 6. [If possible, have a cup of dry rice and dry beans and a scale available for quick measures. Have students round their measures to the nearest ounce.]

One cup of uncooked rice weighs about _____ ounces. [Fill in appropriate amount.] Knowing this, answer the following questions:

One pint of rice weighs about _____ ounces.

One quart of rice weighs about _____ ounces.

One gallon of rice weighs about _____ ounces.

One gallon of rice weighs about _____ pounds.

Would 1 cup of dry beans equal 1 cup of dry rice in capacity? In weight? Explain your thinking. Does the expression in Question 5 hold true?

> This question may help students make a distinction between capacity and weight. A cup is a measure of capacity. A pound is a measure of weight.

 7. Fill in the blanks with numbers so that the story makes sense.

Jacob wonders what happened to his little Chocolate Lab puppy! When he first brought her home, Coffee weighed _____ pounds. Jacob fed Coffee _____ cups of puppy food each day. By the time Coffee was _____ months old, she weighed _____ pounds, _____ pounds more than when Jacob brought her home! Jacob is worried. A full-grown Lab can weigh as much as _____ pounds. Sometime soon, someone needs to tell Coffee that she can no longer be a lapdog!

> Filling in the blanks with the appropriate numbers helps students focus not only on the measurements but on their proper use within a context.

OVERVIEW

Area and Perimeter

(Grades 5–6)

Experiences at This Level Will Help Students To

- understand the importance of standard units
- estimate, make, and use measurements
- compute and compare areas and perimeters of plane figures

Reproducibles are available in a downloadable, printable format. See page xx for directions about how to access them.

Materials

- color tiles
- drawing paper
- Irregular Polygon (Reproducible 27)
- Cutout Polygon Models (Reproducible 28)
- scissors and tape or glue
- Graph Paper (Reproducible A)

Good Questions and Teacher Notes (pages 241–249)

240   GOOD QUESTIONS FOR MATH TEACHING

AREA AND PERIMETER (GRADES 5–6)

 1. Describe two situations in which you want to know the perimeter of something.

Units for perimeter are linear: cm, km, in., ft. Why?

 2. Describe two situations in which you would want to know the area of something.

Units for area are square units (units^2): cm^2, km^2, in.^{2}, ft.^{2}. Why?

 3. Describe two situations in which you would want to know the surface area of something.

Units for surface area are square units (units^2): cm^2, km^2, in.^{2}, ft.^{2}. Why?

> Identifying uses of these measures can help students apply understandings of area, perimeter, and surface area to real-life situations. As students begin to make the connection between the measurement label (whether linear or units^2) and the actual measurement, they will be able to make better sense of procedures used to calculate perimeter, area, and surface area.

GOOD QUESTIONS AND TEACHER NOTES

 4. What could be the dimensions of a rectangle with 20 square units and whole number side lengths that has

   a. the largest perimeter?

   b. the smallest perimeter?

   Explain how you found your answers for both a and b.

   Can you make a generalization about shapes that will give you large perimeters?

   Can you make a generalization about shapes that will give you small perimeters?

   Would these same generalizations work with a rectangle of 100 units²? Explain your thinking.

   Can you think of a real-life situation when the magnitude of the perimeter would matter?

"Skinny" rectangles will give the largest perimeter, which can easily be demonstrated with color tiles. Because the tiles will touch only on one or two edges, many edges are exposed.

If you are bordering a pool or a garden and only have so much money to spend on tiling or edging, then the perimeter measurement would have an impact on the shape of the pool or the garden.

AREA AND PERIMETER (GRADES 5–6)

 5. What could the dimensions be of a rectangle with a perimeter of 16 units and whole number side lengths that has

   a. the largest area?

   b. the smallest area?

   Explain how you found your answers for both a and b.

   Can you make a generalization about shapes with large areas? Can you make a generalization about shapes with small areas?

   Can you think of a real-life situation when the magnitude of the area would matter?

   Would these same generalizations about shapes work with a rectangle that has a perimeter of 100 units?

The rectangle that is most like a square will have the greatest area. Having students build the rectangles with color tiles will help them see the relationship between the shape of the rectangle and the area.

Giving a context to the answer will give greater meaning to the solution. Building a dog pen could be a context in which the area matters.

GOOD QUESTIONS FOR MATH TEACHING

GOOD QUESTIONS AND TEACHER NOTES

6. Rima says her rectangle has a perimeter of 30 units and an area of 50 units^2. Courtney says her rectangle also has a perimeter of 30 units but an area of 56 units^2. Can they both be correct? Explain. Use drawings to support your thinking.

Can you think of a real-life situation when the dimensions of the rectangle would be important?

> Many times, students are convinced that shapes with a given perimeter have the same area. Encourage students to build or draw their shapes as they try to convince each other that Rima's rectangle can be 10 units by 5 units and Courtney's rectangle can be 7 units by 8 units. Giving a context to the answer will give greater meaning to the solution.

7. Kirsten says, "My rectangle has a greater area than yours."

Kai replies, "My rectangle has a greater perimeter than yours."

What might the dimensions of each of their rectangles be?

> Encourage students to draw and label their rectangles. When discussing solutions, be sure to listen for—and address—the misconception that shapes with a larger area have a larger perimeter as well.

AREA AND PERIMETER (GRADES 5–6)

  8. Use two methods to find the area of this figure. Explain both of your methods. Is one more efficient than the other? Why or why not?

(See Reproducible 27, Irregular Polygon.)

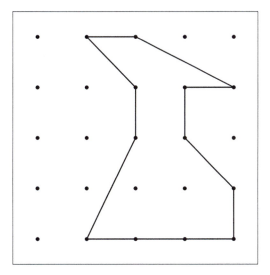

Asking students to compute the area of irregular shapes helps extend their understanding of area and its calculation. Students will begin to realize that area can be constructed in many ways. Although the perimeter may change as the result of the reconfiguration, the area remains constant.

GOOD QUESTIONS FOR MATH TEACHING

GOOD QUESTIONS AND TEACHER NOTES

9. Can you always determine the perimeter of a figure if you know its area?

   Can you determine the area of a figure if you know its perimeter?

   Are area and perimeter related? If so, how?

   > Displaying counterexamples (examples that disprove a "yes" response to either question) can help students see that knowing one measure does not necessarily mean you can determine the other. Although area and perimeter are not directly related, they do tend to put constraints on each other.

10. A rectangle has the same area as a triangle whose area is $24\frac{1}{2}$ square inches. What might the dimensions of the rectangle and the triangle be?

    > Embedding calculation work with fractions within the context of this question offers additional computational practice. Sharing strategies as a class will offer insights into the flexibility of students' manipulation of area computations.

11. What might be the side lengths of a triangle with a perimeter of $18\frac{3}{4}$ inches?

    > When identifying side lengths of a triangle, it is important for students to consider that the sum of any two sides of a triangle must be greater than the third.

AREA AND PERIMETER (GRADES 5–6)

 12. Can you fit a circle with a radius of 2.25 inches inside a circle with a diameter of 5.25 inches? Explain your thinking.

> Students may set about to calculate the areas of the two circles, when, in fact, area measurements are not necessary for answering this question. The relationship between the radius measurement and that of the diameter can help set up an initial response. The relative sizes of the circles can then be addressed.

 13. You have been asked to help change the pricing of pizzas at Pepper Roni's Pizza Parlor. You can price pizza in one of three ways:

Suggestion 1: The price of pizza could be based on its diameter.

Suggestion 2: The price of pizza could be based on its area.

Suggestion 3: The price of pizza could be based on its circumference.

If you were to decide, which suggestion would you adopt? Explain. Give examples of your reasoning.

> Students may wish to calculate the diameter, area, and circumference of a specific-size pizza before they generalize opinions. Remind students that their decisions need to be based on financial proof!

GOOD QUESTIONS FOR MATH TEACHING   247

GOOD QUESTIONS AND TEACHER NOTES

 14. The circumference of each of Malik's bicycle wheels is 50 inches. How many rotations will Malik's wheels make in 1 mile? Explain how you calculated your answer. When would this information matter to Malik?

> Although conversion activities offer students opportunities to practice calculating skills, conversion charts and calculators may help students focus on the process of conversion rather than just on the calculation.

 15. What happens to the area of a square when its dimensions are doubled? Tripled?

Does the same pattern hold true for a rectangle? How about a triangle?

Use cutout models to represent your reasoning. Create a chart to record your measurements.

(See Reproducible 28, Cutout Polygon Models.)

> Be prepared for many misconceptions as students work to answer this question! Students will likely assume that doubling the dimensions can be equated to doubling the area, when in fact the new area is four times greater! The same misconceptions may occur when students think about tripling the dimensions.

AREA AND PERIMETER (GRADES 5–6)

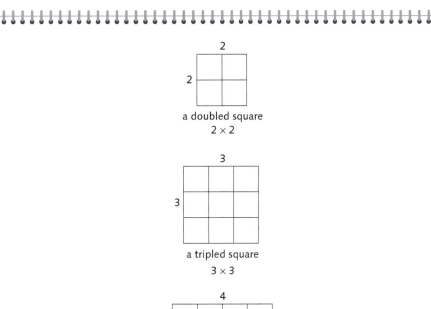

a doubled square
2 × 2

a tripled square
3 × 3

a quadrupled square
4 × 4

Have students answer the following questions for homework: What happens to the area of a square when you quadruple the dimensions? Does the same hold true for a rectangle? How about a triangle? Can you generalize a rule to predict the area of a square, rectangle, or triangle when its dimensions are increased any number (*n*) of times?

OVERVIEW

VOLUME (GRADES 5–6)

EXPERIENCES AT THIS LEVEL WILL HELP STUDENTS TO

- understand the importance of standard units
- estimate, make, and use measurements
- compute and compare the volume of three-dimensional shapes

Reproducibles are available in a downloadable, printable format. See page xx for directions about how to access them.

MATERIALS

- Volume Pattern (Reproducible 29)
- linking or Unifix cubes
- Prisms (Reproducible 30)
- Graph Paper (Reproducible A)

GOOD QUESTIONS AND TEACHER NOTES (PAGES 251–256)

250   GOOD QUESTIONS FOR MATH TEACHING

VOLUME (GRADES 5–6)

1. Continuing the pattern in these figures, what will be the volume of Figure 4? Figure 10? Figure 100? Explain your thinking.

   Can you create a rule to determine the volume of any figure that follows this pattern?

   (See Reproducible 29, Volume Pattern.)

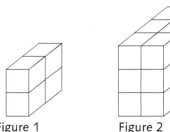
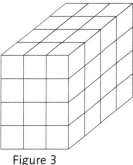

Figure 1
4 units
1 × 2 × 2

Figure 2
18 units
2 × 3 × 3

Figure 3
48 units
3 × 4 × 4

Having students build the prisms with Unifix or linking cubes will help them see the pattern of growth. Encourage partner talk as the students build the prisms.

Students may find it helpful to chart the growth of the prisms. If they choose to do so, it is important that they can identify each number and what it represents and where it is on the prism. Asking students to predict the volume of Figures 10 and 100 will help them develop the ability to generalize a rule from a pattern.

GOOD QUESTIONS FOR MATH TEACHING

GOOD QUESTIONS AND TEACHER NOTES

 2. Estimate the length, width, and height of the following objects. Chart your estimations. What unit of measure will you use for each estimate?

   a. your desk/table

   b. a filing cabinet

   c. a dictionary

   d. a whiteboard/chalkboard eraser

   e. your classroom

Check your estimates against another classmate's. What range of measurement would you consider to be accurate? What would be a reasonable margin of error?

> Determining an acceptable margin of error can lead to many interesting class discussions. Measurement is approximate by its nature. Students may determine that being off by an inch is OK for one item but not OK for another.

 3. Fill in the blanks with numbers so that this story makes sense.

Bali is making a batch of sugar 'n' spice cookies for his math class. His recipe will make _____ dozen, or _____ cookies. The recipe calls for _____ cups of molasses and _____ cups of flour among other ingredients. Bali is to bake the cookies for _____ minutes in a _____° oven.

> Filling in the blanks with the appropriate numbers helps students focus not only on the measurements but on their proper use within a context.

252 GOOD QUESTIONS FOR MATH TEACHING

VOLUME (GRADES 5–6)

4. Farhad uses ten blocks to build a four-step staircase. How many blocks will he need for a twelve-step staircase? How do you know? Create a number model to represent your answer.

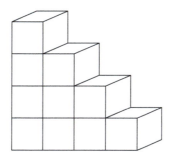

Some students may need to build staircases to help them predict the number of blocks in a twelve-step staircase. Others may use the four-step staircase and extrapolate the numbers from that diagram alone.

5. Describe two situations in which you would want to know the volume of something.

Units for volume are units^3 — cm^3, in.^{3} Why? How does this compare with what you know about perimeter and area measures?

Volume is a measure of the amount of space occupied by a three-dimensional object. As students begin to make the connection between the measurement label (units^3) and actual measurement, they will be able to make better sense of procedures used to calculate volume.

GOOD QUESTIONS FOR MATH TEACHING   253

GOOD QUESTIONS AND TEACHER NOTES

6. Select the number set that indicates the most likely dimensions of each prism. The volume is given.

   (See Reproducible 30, Prisms.)

   a. 4, 6, 10   d. 3, 3, 9   f. 5, 2, 15
   b. 2, 10, 10   e. 3, 5, 9   g. 2, 5, 8
   c. 5, 5, 5

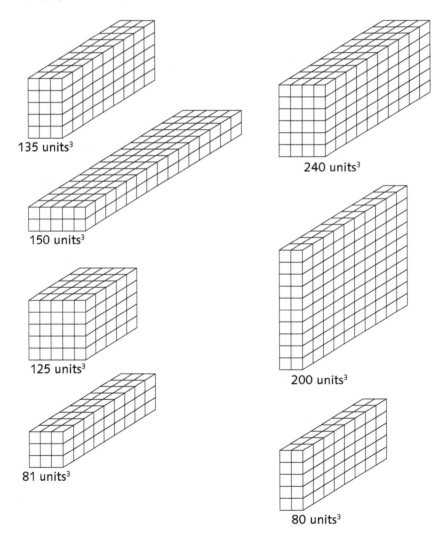

VOLUME (GRADES 5–6)

Although calculating the volume of the lettered dimensions could result in correct matching, determining what measurements could *not* be matched with a specific figure using reasoning and logical thinking can also be employed. For example, c cannot be matched to 150 units^3 because all of the dimensions of c are the same. The figure with a volume of 150 units^3 does not have any dimensions of equal length.

GOOD QUESTIONS AND TEACHER NOTES

 7. A packaging factory wants you to build a box that will hold twice as many cubes as the box pictured here:

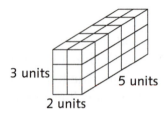

What could the dimensions of the new box be? How do you know? Draw your new box to scale using graph paper.

(See Reproducible A, Graph Paper.)

> Students are asked to double the volume, *not* to double the dimensions. Some students may not realize that there is a difference between these two ideas.
>
> After completing this investigation, ask students to answer the following questions: What happens to the volume of the original box when the *dimensions* are doubled? Is the volume of this box the same as the doubled volume of the original box?
>
> What would happen to the dimensions of the box if it needed to hold four times as many cubes? Eight times as many cubes? Can you identify a pattern? What also happens to the surface area as the volumes of all the boxes increase?
>
> Creating T-charts will help students to chart the progressions of the volume as well as the surface area. Charting the growth will also help students to identify patterns and to make generalizations.

OVERVIEW

WEIGHT (Grades 7–8)

Experiences at This Level Will Help Students To

- weigh and estimate weights of common objects
- convert within and between systems of measurement
- choose appropriate units of weight for particular objects
- use known weights to estimate unknown weights
- relate weight to other attributes of objects (such as volume and area)

Materials

- items weighing 1 gram, 1 kilogram, and 1 pound
- balance scales and spring scales
- flour
- measuring cups
- popped and unpopped popcorn
- coins

Good Questions and Teacher Notes (pages 258–260)

GOOD QUESTIONS FOR MATH TEACHING   257

GOOD QUESTIONS AND TEACHER NOTES

1. Identify two objects where one weighs less but has greater volume than the other.

> Introduce the term *density* when discussing this question.

2. Which unit(s) of measure would be most appropriate to measure the weight of each of the following items:

   a. a pillow

   b. a puppy

   c. a textbook

   d. a sofa

> The ability to determine a suitable unit of measurement is a very important measurement skill.

3. Think of objects whose weights you would measure in each of the following units:

   a. grams

   b. kilograms

   c. pounds

   d. tons

> To help students answer this question, have items available that weigh 1 gram, 1 kilogram, and 1 pound. Also, you may wish to tell students that 1 ton equals 2,000 pounds. Students can use the weights of these items to estimate the weights of others.

WEIGHT (GRADES 7–8)

 4. I went shopping and found a 1-pound box of Snowflake Sugar Cubes for $2.70. A 1-kilogram box of White Cloud Sugar Cubes offered a better buy. How much might the White Cloud Sugar Cubes have cost?

> Give students the conversion (1 pound ≈ 0.454 kilogram) so that they can estimate a possible price by reasoning that 1 pound is about the same as half of 1 kilogram.

 5. A medium-size cat weighs 6 kilograms. Use this information to estimate the weights of other animals.

> This question develops students' ability to reason proportionally. For example, a fully-grown Saint Bernard is about ten times the size of a medium-size cat, so it probably weighs about 60 kilograms. A cow is about one hundred times the size of a medium-size cat, so it could weigh 600 kilograms. This question can be reused with another benchmark weight and unit (e.g., pounds or grams).

 6. Sheila emptied her piggy bank and put the coins in a bag to bring to the bank. The bag weighed 5 pounds. How much money do you think Sheila had in coins?

> In order to answer this question, students will need to estimate or determine the weight of different types and numbers of coins. You may provide students with these items or have them find the information for themselves.

GOOD QUESTIONS FOR MATH TEACHING   259

GOOD QUESTIONS AND TEACHER NOTES

7. White's Bakery uses 30-pound bags of flour. Its triple-layer cake uses 4 cups of flour. How many cups of flour do you think are in one bag of flour?

> In order to answer this question, students will need to estimate or find the weight of smaller amounts of flour. To help them with this, you may wish to provide materials such as measuring cups, flour, and a spring scale. As a follow-up question, ask, "How many triple-layer cakes could be baked with the flour in one whole bag?"

8. I bought medium-size packing boxes that each hold 20 kilograms to move to a new house. What objects might I put in one of these boxes?

> Since this question requires students to think about the weights of household objects, they may need to explore this question for homework. In addition, you may wish to provide them with the equivalence between pounds and kilograms to help them estimate the weights of various objects in kilograms.

9. Unpopped popcorn kernels are on one side of a balance scale and popped popcorn is on the other. How many of each might be on each side if the scale is level?

> Students could find the weight of a group of kernels and a few handfuls of popped popcorn rather than the weight of each piece (since individual kernels and pieces of popcorn are so light).

OVERVIEW

AREA (GRADES 7–8)

EXPERIENCES AT THIS LEVEL WILL HELP STUDENTS TO

- estimate and measure the area of two-dimensional shapes and the surface area of three-dimensional shapes
- select appropriate units from both systems of measurement
- relate area to other attributes of a shape, such as side length
- use known areas to estimate unknown areas

Reproducibles are available in a downloadable, printable format. See page xx for directions about how to access them.

MATERIALS

- 11-by-17-inch pieces of paper
- geoboard or Dot Paper (Reproducible B)
- Graph Paper (Reproducible A)

GOOD QUESTIONS AND TEACHER NOTES (PAGES 262–264)

GOOD QUESTIONS FOR MATH TEACHING   261

GOOD QUESTIONS AND TEACHER NOTES

1. I wrapped a rectangular box in a piece of wrapping paper that was 11 inches by 17 inches. I had no paper left over but did have some minor overlaps. What might have been the dimensions of my box?

> Have 11-by-17-inch paper available to help students answer this question. This question can be extended by giving the size of a present to be wrapped and then asking students what size sheet of wrapping paper would cover it.

2. Find the length, width, and height of a rectangular prism that has a surface area of more than 200 square inches but less than 300 square inches.

> It will be interesting for students to discuss how they answered this question. Some students may choose to draw labeled sketches of the prism while others may choose to work directly with a formula for surface area.

3. A ball of dough is rolled out into a circle with a 12-inch diameter. How many cookies with a diameter of 2.5 inches can be made from this dough?

> Some students may wish to answer this question by applying the area formula for circles—figuring out the area of the ball of dough, figuring out the area of each cookie, and dividing (assuming that all the dough is used up). Some other students may choose a visual approach wherein they draw a scaled picture of the dough and divide it into cookies that are also drawn to scale.

AREA (GRADES 7–8)

 4. A rectangle is approximately equal in area to a circle whose area is 49π square inches. What might be the length and width of this rectangle?

> Watch for students who equate 49π square inches with 49 square inches.

 5. Circle A has an area of 9π square units. Circle B has an area of 16π square units. Find the side length of a square whose area is greater than that of Circle A but less than that of Circle B.

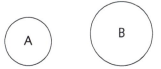

> Students sometimes have difficulty interpreting measurements such as 9π and 16π. You may wish to discuss what these measurements mean before posing this question. One way to answer this question is to think of a square that is *circumscribed* around Circle A. Since Circle A must have a radius of 3 units, the square would have a side length of 6 units and an area of 36 square units, which is more than 9π but less than 16π.

 6. A banquet hall can seat 150 to 200 people. How big might this banquet hall be?

> One way to get started answering this question is to figure out how many people will sit at each table, how big that table will be, and how much space will separate each table. Then, apply proportional reasoning to estimate the size of the room.

GOOD QUESTIONS FOR MATH TEACHING   263

GOOD QUESTIONS AND TEACHER NOTES

 7. I drew an irregular eight-sided figure on a blank piece of paper. Only five sides were marked but that was still enough information to figure out the area of the entire figure. What might this figure have looked like?

> It might help students to sketch their figures on graph paper before transferring to blank paper. (See Reproducible A, Graph Paper.) Note whether students use symmetry and/or right angles to create their figures. As a follow-up question, ask students to find the perimeters of their figures.

 8. A roll of wallpaper is 1 meter by 10 meters. How many rolls do you think would be needed to cover the walls of this classroom?

> Decide whether students will measure or estimate the area of the walls of the classroom.

 9. Create a square on a geoboard or geoboard dot paper whose area is not a square number. How long is each side of your square?

(See Reproducible B, Dot Paper.)

> The side length of the square will be the square root of area of the square.

264 GOOD QUESTIONS FOR MATH TEACHING

OVERVIEW

LENGTH AND PERIMETER

(GRADES 7–8)

EXPERIENCES AT THIS LEVEL WILL HELP STUDENTS TO

- solve problems about side lengths and perimeters of polygons and radii and circumferences of circles
- use the Pythagorean theorem to find linear measurements
- reason proportionally to solve problems about linear measurement

Reproducibles are available in a downloadable, printable format. See page xx for directions about how to access them.

MATERIALS

- geoboards or Dot Paper (Reproducible B)
- rulers, meter sticks, and yardsticks
- Graph Paper (Reproducible A)

GOOD QUESTIONS AND TEACHER NOTES (PAGES 266–270)

GOOD QUESTIONS FOR MATH TEACHING   265

GOOD QUESTIONS AND TEACHER NOTES

1. A string is used to form a circle whose circumference is 36π centimeters. If the string is then reformed to create a rectangle, what might be its length and width?

> Watch for students who equate 36π centimeters with 36 centimeters.

2. One-centimeter-wide ribbon is wrapped around a spool that has a radius of 4 centimeters and a height of 12 centimeters. There are approximately three layers of ribbon wrapped around the spool. What might be the length in meters of the entire piece of ribbon?

> Be sure to allow plenty of time to discuss this complex question that requires integrated knowledge of circumference, spatial visualization, linear measurement, and estimation.

3. A piece of art is hung in a rectangular frame that measures approximately 41 inches along its diagonal. What might be the length and width of the frame?

> Finding the length and width of a rectangular object using the measure of its diagonal is a real-life application of the Pythagorean theorem. As a follow-up to this question, have students find print advertisements of other items measured by their diagonals (e.g., a computer screen) and use them to reason about their lengths and widths.

LENGTH AND PERIMETER (GRADES 7–8)

 4. A 15-foot-tall ladder has a warning that reads "Bottom of ladder should rest between 3 and 4 feet from the wall." What are some heights that a person standing on the ladder can reach?

> Drawing a picture of the ladder leaning against a wall might help students see this question as an application of the Pythagorean theorem.

 5. Create a right triangle on a geoboard or on dot paper whose perimeter is more than 5 units but less than 10 units.

(See Reproducible B, Dot Paper.)

> Asking students to find the perimeters of non-right triangles can be a useful extension to this question.

 6. If we wanted to draw a floor map of our classroom on an 8.5-by-11-inch piece of paper, what might be our scale?

> You can extend this question by asking students to think of a scale that would allow them to draw the floor map of the school on an 8.5-by-11-inch piece of paper.

GOOD QUESTIONS FOR MATH TEACHING

GOOD QUESTIONS AND TEACHER NOTES

7. If all of the students in this school arrived at once and entered the building in a single-file line, how long do you think this line would be?

> One way to answer this question is to estimate the length of a single-file line for the students in one class and use proportional reasoning to estimate the length of a line for all the classes in the school.
>
> For homework, ask students to investigate other scaling problems that are meaningful to them. For example, students might investigate the capacity of the bleachers at their school's football stadium and provide a linear benchmark for that number.

8. Kara thinks that when both the length and the width of a rectangle are doubled, the perimeter is doubled. Than disagrees. He thinks that the perimeter will get four times bigger since that is what happens to the area. Whom do you agree with? Why?

> Pose this question after students have explored the relationship between scale factor and change in area. The fact that the perimeter doubles when the area quadruples is a common source of confusion for students. Spending time discussing why this makes sense will deepen students' understanding of perimeter as a linear measurement and area as a two-dimensional measurement.

LENGTH AND PERIMETER (GRADES 7–8)

 9. Use graph paper or dot paper to measure a length that can only be expressed as an irrational number.

Write the length of the line you drew.

(See Reproducible A, Graph Paper and Reproducible B, Dot Paper.)

> Once students find one possible length, ask them to deduce the lengths of lines that are two, three, four, or *n* times as long.

 10. A round banquet table seats 10 people comfortably. What might be the diameter (in feet) of this table?

> One way to answer this question is to estimate the length one person needs to be seated comfortably, multiply that number by 10, use the product as the circumference of the table, and derive the diameter using $C = \pi d$ (e.g., if each person needs 2 feet → $2 \times 10 = 20$; $20 = \pi d$; $d \approx 6.4$ feet).

 11. The perimeter of a right triangle is approximately 25 units. What might be its three side lengths?

> Be sure students' answers satisfy the Pythagorean Theorem *and* the triangle inequality theorem (the sum of any two side lengths must be greater than the third).

GOOD QUESTIONS FOR MATH TEACHING

GOOD QUESTIONS AND TEACHER NOTES

 12. Explain how to use the Pythagorean Theorem to find the perimeter of the grey region inside the 8-cm-by-15-cm rectangle sketched here.

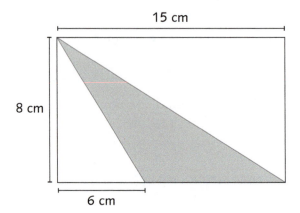

> Students may be quite facile using the Pythagorean Theorem to find the measures of right triangles but struggle to see its relevance here given that the triangle in question is not a right triangle. If necessary, scaffold this question by first asking students to identify all the triangles they see within the figure.

OVERVIEW

Volume and Capacity

(Grades 7–8)

Experiences at This Level Will Help Students To

- solve problems about the volume of three-dimensional shapes
- use appropriate units of measure for problems about volume and liquid capacity

Materials

- blank paper
- calibrated measuring cups or prisms
- common food items
- milk and juice cartons and/or three-dimensional models of prisms, pyramids, and polyhedrons

Good Questions and Teacher Notes (pages 272–275)

GOOD QUESTIONS FOR MATH TEACHING   271

GOOD QUESTIONS AND TEACHER NOTES

1. How are the methods of finding the volumes of polygonal prisms and cylinders similar and different?

> This type of compare-and-contrast question will help students connect what they are learning about volumes of different three-dimensional shapes rather than see each idea in isolation. For example, the formula "volume equals base times height" can be used for any polygonal prism and cylinder, *but* the methods for finding the area of the base vary according to the shape of the base.

2. A prism has approximately the same volume as a cylinder with a volume of 24π cubic inches. What might be the dimensions of this prism?

> Watch for students who equate 24π cubic inches with 24 cubic inches.

3. The surface area of a cylinder is between 200π and 300π square inches. What might be its volume?

> This is a complex question that takes many steps to answer. Reasoning through a question that incorporates both surface area and volume will strengthen students' understanding of each.

VOLUME AND CAPACITY (GRADES 7–8)

4. A cylinder holds exactly ninety-six cubes with a side length of 1 inch. What might be the dimensions of this cylinder?

> Be sure to discuss at least one answer that approximates the value of π and one that gives the answer in terms of π.

5. Take four pieces of letter-size (8.5-by-11-inch) paper. Fold the papers into one tall and one short square prism and one tall and one short cylinder. Predict and then determine whether the volumes will be the same or different (Burns 2000).

> Many students predict that all four objects will have the same volume since all four pieces of paper are the same size. Volume, however, is not a function of surface area but rather the area of the base and the height of the container.

6. Could $1,000,000 actually fit into a standard-size briefcase? Assume the largest denomination in circulation is $100.

> Since a black briefcase full of money is often a common feature on television and in the movies, students will enjoy the opportunity to verify or refute the claim of the $1,000,000 contents.

GOOD QUESTIONS FOR MATH TEACHING   273

GOOD QUESTIONS AND TEACHER NOTES

 7. The cylinder shown here holds three standard-size tennis balls. What do you notice and what do you wonder about the cylinder?

Students' answers might include approximations of the diameter of each tennis ball based on the height of the cylinder.

 8. You write on paper every day in school. If you were to box up all of the pieces of paper you've used since entering school, what fraction of this room do you think the boxes would fill?

To begin answering this question, students must estimate the size of the boxes they would use, how many papers would fit in one of these boxes, and how many papers they've written on in a typical year in school.

VOLUME AND CAPACITY (GRADES 7–8)

9. Our school cafeteria sells cartons of milk and cans of juice. Estimate how many milliliters of liquid are sold each week.

> Adapt this question so that it reflects the type(s) and container(s) of liquids sold in your school's cafeteria. Have samples of these containers and/or calibrated measuring cups or prisms available to help students with their estimates. As a follow-up question, ask, "What size refrigerator is needed to hold a week's worth?"

10. One cubic centimeter of water weighs 1 gram. One thousand cubic centimeters equal 1 liter. Use this to estimate the weight of other objects when they are full of water: a fish bowl, a fish tank, a children's pool, a watering can, and so on.

> Students will need to estimate the capacity of these objects and then use proportional reasoning to estimate their weights.

11. Cylinder A and Cylinder B are equal in volume but are not identical. What might be the radius and height of each cylinder?

> You might ask students to represent the radius and height of each cylinder using variables instead of specific measures. For example, if the radius of Cylinder A is r and the height is h, the volume of Cylinder A is $\pi r^2 h$. Then, if the radius of Cylinder B is $2r$ and the height is $\frac{1}{4}h$, the volume of Cylinder B is also $\pi r^2 h$; $V = \pi(2r)^2 \frac{1}{4}h = \pi 4r^2 \frac{1}{4}h = \pi r^2 h$.
>
> Extend this question by asking students to generalize about the measures of any Cylinder B in terms of the measures of Cylinder A (e.g., If the radius of Cylinder A is r and the height is h, the radius of Cylinder B is ar and the height is $\frac{1}{a^2}$).

GOOD QUESTIONS FOR MATH TEACHING

REPRODUCIBLES

The following reproducibles are referenced throughout the text. These reproducibles are also available in a downloadable, printable format. For access, visit http://hein.pub/MathOLR and register your product using the key code **GQ58**. See page xx for more detailed instructions.

Reproducible 1	Fair Game 2
Reproducible 2	Pattern Block Figure
Reproducible 3	Grid Figure
Reproducible 4	Fractions Dot Paper
Reproducible 5	6-by-6-Inch Template
Reproducible 6	Tenths and Hundredths Grids
Reproducible 7	Hundredths Grid
Reproducible 8	∠HAT
Reproducible 9	Clock Faces
Reproducible 10	Polygon Sets
Reproducible 11	Polygon Venn Diagram and Shape Bank
Reproducible 12	Polygon Venn Diagram (Extension)

(Continued)

Reproducible 13	Rectangle ABCD
Reproducible 14	Number Path A
Reproducible 15	Number Path B
Reproducible 16	Patio Borders
Reproducible 17	Pencil Sharpener Stories and Graphs
Reproducible 18	As Time Goes By Graphs
Reproducible 19	Grouping Patterns
Reproducible 20	Walk-a-Thon Graphs
Reproducible 21	Perimeter and Area Tables
Reproducible 22	Mystery Line Plots
Reproducible 23	Investment Graphs
Reproducible 24	Dart Board
Reproducible 25	Bags of Marbles
Reproducible 26	Weights
Reproducible 27	Irregular Polygon
Reproducible 28	Cutout Polygon Models
Reproducible 29	Volume Pattern
Reproducible 30	Prisms

The following reproducibles are referenced and used throughout the book:

Reproducible A	Graph Paper
Reproducible B	Dot Paper
Reproducible C	Blank Spinner Faces

REPRODUCIBLE 1

Fair Game 2

You need: a partner
             a pair of dice

Rules

Take turns rolling the two dice. Player A scores a point if the sum is even. Player B scores a point if the sum is odd. Is the game fair? If not, how could you make the game fair? Explain your reasoning.

Play the game again, this time figuring out the product. Player A scores a point if the product is even. Player B scores a point if the product is odd. Is the game fair? If not, how could you make the game fair? Explain your reasoning.

For use with Chapter 4, Question 4, section Grades 5–6: Even and Odd.
From *Good Questions for Math Teaching, Grades 5–8, Second Edition*, by Lainie Schuster and Nancy Anderson. Portsmouth, NH: Heinemann. © 2020 by Heinemann. May be photocopied for classroom use.

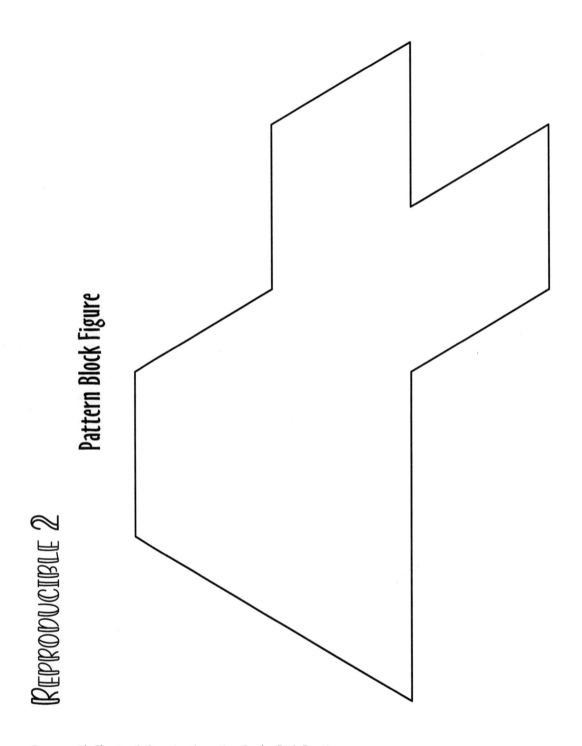

Reproducible 2: Pattern Block Figure

For use with Chapter 6, Question 1, section Grades 5–6: Fractions.

From *Good Questions for Math Teaching, Grades 5–8, Second Edition*, by Lainie Schuster and Nancy Anderson. Portsmouth, NH: Heinemann. © 2020 by Heinemann. May be photocopied for classroom use.

Reproducible 3

Grid Figure

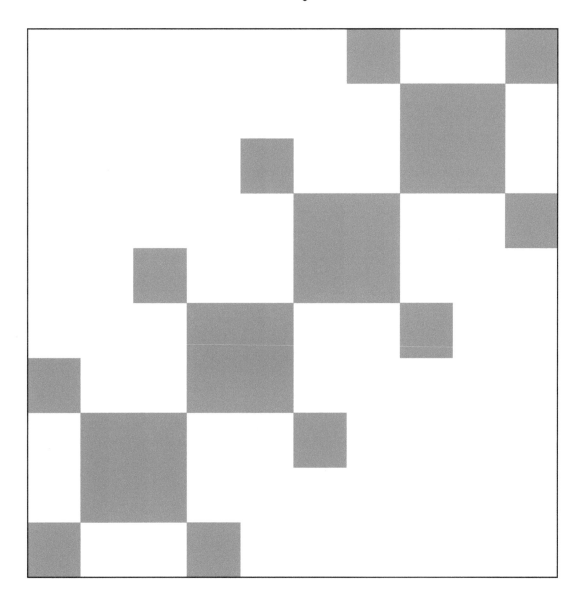

For use with Chapter 6, Question 4, section Grades 5–6: Fractions.
From *Good Questions for Math Teaching, Grades 5–8, Second Edition*, by Lainie Schuster and Nancy Anderson. Portsmouth, NH: Heinemann. © 2020 by Heinemann. May be photocopied for classroom use.

REPRODUCIBLE 4

Fractions Dot Paper

For use with Chapter 6, Question 7, section Grades 5–6: Fractions.

From *Good Questions for Math Teaching, Grades 5–8, Second Edition*, by Lainie Schuster and Nancy Anderson. Portsmouth, NH: Heinemann. © 2020 by Heinemann. May be photocopied for classroom use.

Reproducible 5

6-by-6-Inch Template

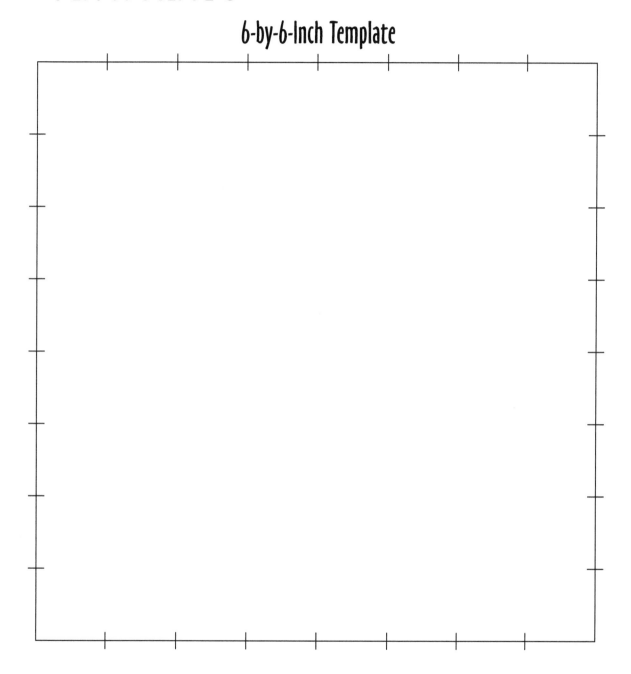

For use with Chapter 6, Question 8, section Grades 5–6: Fractions.
From *Good Questions for Math Teaching, Grades 5–8, Second Edition*, by Lainie Schuster and Nancy Anderson. Portsmouth, NH: Heinemann. © 2020 by Heinemann. May be photocopied for classroom use.

Reproducible 6

Tenths and Hundredths Grid

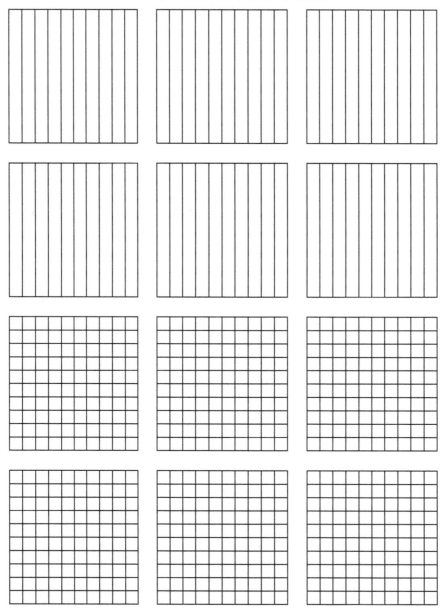

For use with Chapter 6, Question 1, section Grades 5–6: Decimals.
From *Good Questions for Math Teaching, Grades 5–8, Second Edition*, by Lainie Schuster and Nancy Anderson. Portsmouth, NH: Heinemann. © 2020 by Heinemann. May be photocopied for classroom use.

Reproducible 7

Hundredths Grid

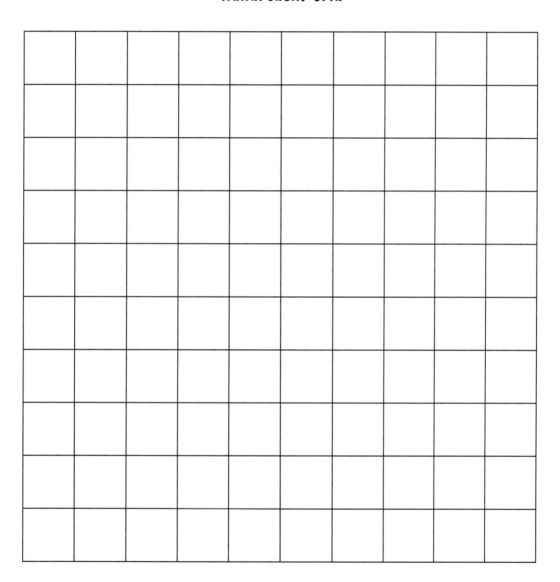

For use with Chapter 6, Question 2, section Grades 5–6: Decimals *and* Question 2, section Grades 5–6: Percentages.
From *Good Questions for Math Teaching, Grades 5–8, Second Edition*, by Lainie Schuster and Nancy Anderson. Portsmouth, NH: Heinemann. © 2020 by Heinemann. May be photocopied for classroom use.

Reproducible 8

∠HAT

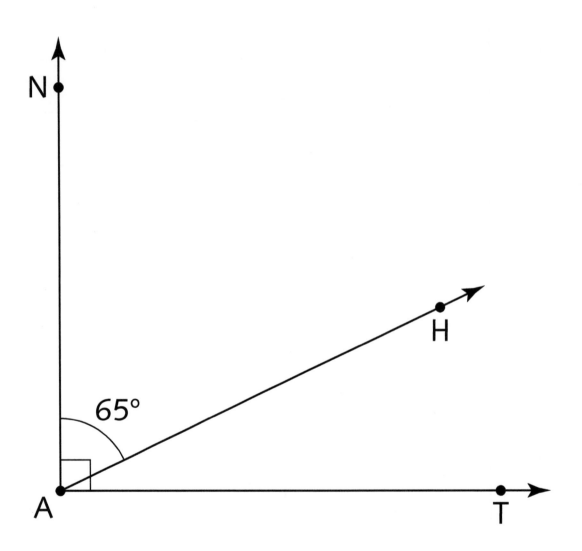

For use with Chapter 7, Question 4, section Grades 5–6: Two-Dimensional Shapes.
From *Good Questions for Math Teaching, Grades 5–8, Second Edition*, by Lainie Schuster and Nancy Anderson. Portsmouth, NH: Heinemann. © 2020 by Heinemann. May be photocopied for classroom use.

REPRODUCIBLE 9

Clock Faces

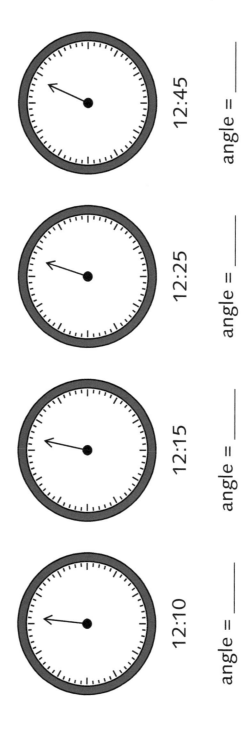

Reproducible 10

Polygon Sets

Set A

Set B

Set C

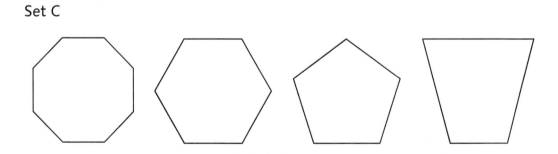

For use with Chapter 7, Question 10, section Grades 5–6: Two-Dimensional Shapes.
From *Good Questions for Math Teaching, Grades 5–8, Second Edition*, by Lainie Schuster and Nancy Anderson. Portsmouth, NH: Heinemann. © 2020 by Heinemann. May be photocopied for classroom use.

Reproducible 11

Polygon Venn Diagram and Shape Bank

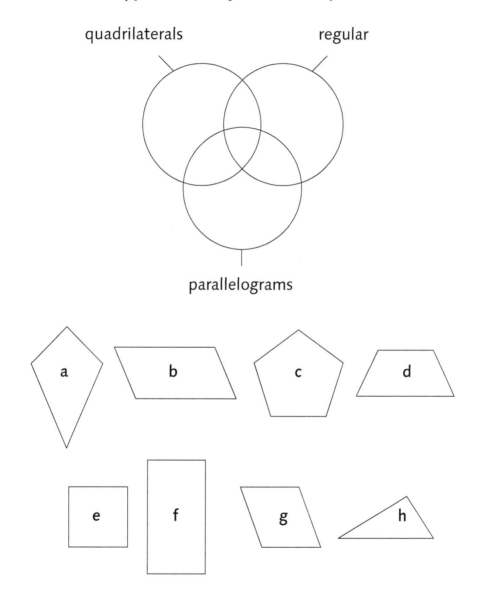

For use with Chapter 7, Question 13, section Grades 5–6: Two-Dimensional Shapes.
From *Good Questions for Math Teaching, Grades 5–8, Second Edition*, by Lainie Schuster and Nancy Anderson. Portsmouth, NH: Heinemann. © 2020 by Heinemann. May be photocopied for classroom use.

289

Reproducible 12

Polygon Venn Diagram (Extension)

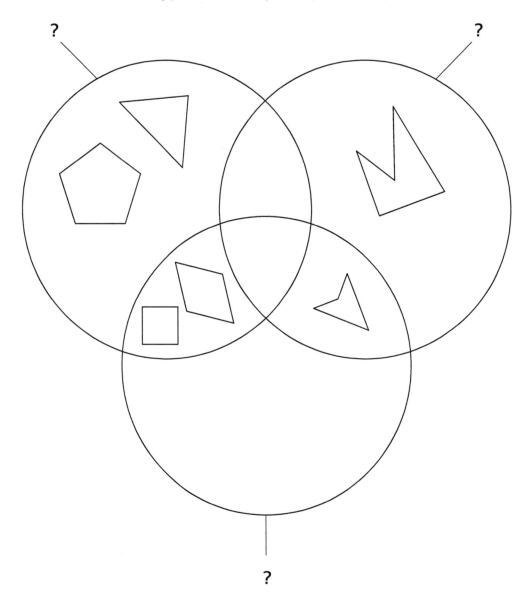

For use with Chapter 7, Question 13, section Grades 5–6: Two-Dimensional Shapes.
From *Good Questions for Math Teaching, Grades 5–8, Second Edition*, by Lainie Schuster and Nancy Anderson. Portsmouth, NH: Heinemann. © 2020 by Heinemann. May be photocopied for classroom use.

Reproducible 13

Rectangle ABCD

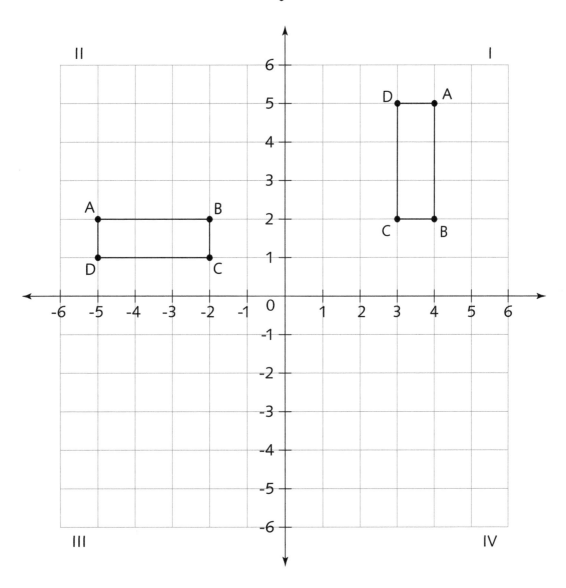

For use with Chapter 7, Question 6, section Grades 7–8: Two-Dimensional Shapes.
From *Good Questions for Math Teaching, Grades 5–8, Second Edition*, by Lainie Schuster and Nancy Anderson. Portsmouth, NH: Heinemann. © 2020 by Heinemann. May be photocopied for classroom use.

Reproducible 14

Number Path A

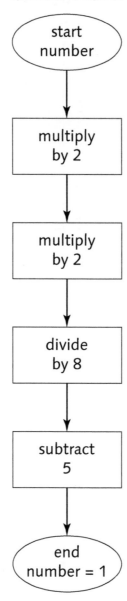

For use with Chapter 8, Question 7, section Grades 5–6: Algebraic Thinking.
From *Good Questions for Math Teaching, Grades 5–8, Second Edition*, by Lainie Schuster and Nancy Anderson. Portsmouth, NH: Heinemann. © 2020 by Heinemann. May be photocopied for classroom use.

Reproducible 15

Number Path B

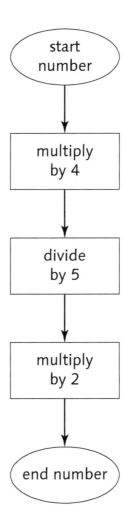

For use with Chapter 8, Question 8, section Grades 5–6: Algebraic Thinking.
From *Good Questions for Math Teaching, Grades 5–8, Second Edition*, by Lainie Schuster and Nancy Anderson. Portsmouth, NH: Heinemann. © 2020 by Heinemann. May be photocopied for classroom use.

Reproducible 16

Patio Borders

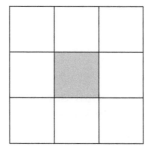

Patio 1: 1 shaded
8 white

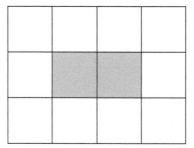

Patio 2: 2 shaded
10 white

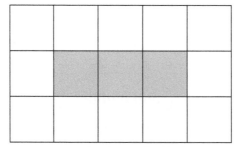

Patio 3: 3 shaded
12 white

For use with Chapter 8, Question 19, section Grades 5–6: Algebraic Thinking.
From *Good Questions for Math Teaching, Grades 5–8, Second Edition,* by Lainie Schuster and Nancy Anderson. Portsmouth, NH: Heinemann. © 2020 by Heinemann. May be photocopied for classroom use.

Reproducible 17

Pencil Sharpener Stories and Graphs

Story A	You get up. Walk toward the pencil sharpener. Stop to answer a question at Molly's table. Walk on to the pencil sharpener. Sharpen your pencil. Walk back to your table.

Story B	You get up. Walk to the pencil sharpener. Sharpen your pencil. Walk back. On the way back, you drop your pencil and break its point. Stop and laugh with Avel. Pick up pencil. Walk back to the pencil sharpener to resharpen the pencil.

Graph 1

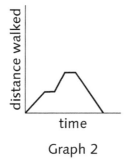

Graph 2

Graph 3

For use with Chapter 8, Question 20, section Grades 5–6: Algebraic Thinking.
From *Good Questions for Math Teaching, Grades 5–8, Second Edition*, by Lainie Schuster and Nancy Anderson. Portsmouth, NH: Heinemann. © 2020 by Heinemann. May be photocopied for classroom use.

Reproducible 18
As Time Goes By Graphs

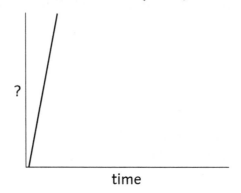

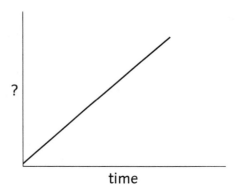

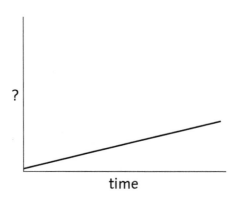

For use with Chapter 8, Question 23, section Grades 5–6: Algebraic Thinking.
From *Good Questions for Math Teaching, Grades 5–8, Second Edition,* by Lainie Schuster and Nancy Anderson. Portsmouth, NH: Heinemann. © 2020 by Heinemann. May be photocopied for classroom use.

REPRODUCIBLE 19

Grouping Patterns

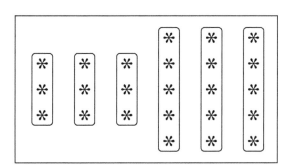
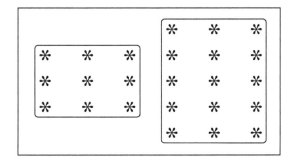

For use with Chapter 8, Question 24, section Grades 5–6: Algebraic Thinking.
From *Good Questions for Math Teaching, Grades 5–8, Second Edition*, by Lainie Schuster and Nancy Anderson. Portsmouth, NH: Heinemann. © 2020 by Heinemann. May be photocopied for classroom use.

Reproducible 20

Walk-a-Thon Graphs

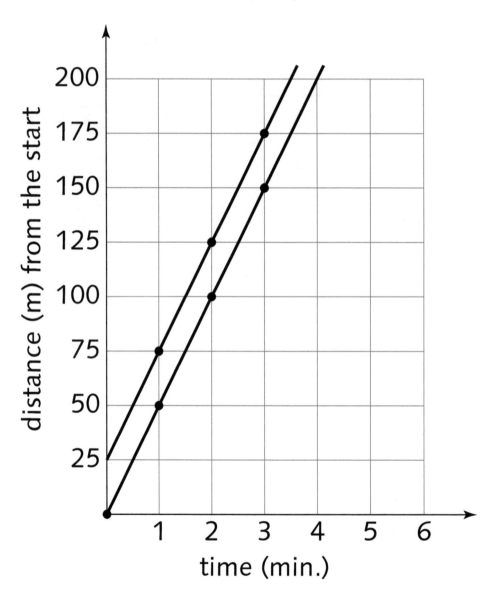

For use with Chapter 8, Question 5, section Grades 7–8: Algebraic Thinking.
From *Good Questions for Math Teaching, Grades 5–8, Second Edition*, by Lainie Schuster and Nancy Anderson. Portsmouth, NH: Heinemann. © 2020 by Heinemann. May be photocopied for classroom use.

REPRODUCIBLE 21

Perimeter and Area Tables

Side Length	Perimeter
1	4
2	8
3	12
10	40

Side Length	Area
1	1
2	4
3	9
10	100

For use with Chapter 8, Question 13, section Grades 7–8: Algebraic Thinking.

From *Good Questions for Math Teaching, Grades 5–8, Second Edition*, by Lainie Schuster and Nancy Anderson. Portsmouth, NH: Heinemann. © 2020 by Heinemann. May be photocopied for classroom use.

Reproducible 22
Mystery Line Plots

```
                        X
              X   X   X
              X   X   X   X       X       X
       X          X   X   X   X   X   X   X       X       X
   ─────────────────────────────────────────────────────────────
   52  53  54  55  56  57  58  59  60  61  62  63  64  65  66  67  68  69  70  71
```
Plot 1

```
                                      X
                  X       X   X       X       X
   X          X       X       X   X       X       X       X   X   X
   ───────────────────────────────────────────────────────────────
   48  50  52  54  56  58  60  62  64  66  68  70  72  74  76  78  80  82
```
Plot 2

```
        X
   X    X
   X    X    X
   X    X    X
   X    X    X    X    X    X    X
   ──────────────────────────────
   0    1    2    3    4    5    6
```
Plot 3

```
                        X
                   X    X        X        X
        X      X       X   X   X   X      X      X        X
   ─────────────────────────────────────────────────────────
   26  28  30  32  34  36  38  40  42  44  46  48  50  52  54
```
Plot 4

```
                        X
            X           X            X    X
   X        X    X      X    X       X    X              X
   ──────────────────────────────────────────────────────
   0    1    2    3    4    5    6    7    8    9    10
```
Plot 5

For use with Chapter 9, Question 7, section Grades 5–6: Data Analysis.

From *Good Questions for Math Teaching, Grades 5–8, Second Edition*, by Lainie Schuster and Nancy Anderson. Portsmouth, NH: Heinemann. © 2020 by Heinemann. May be photocopied for classroom use.

Reproducible 23

Investment Graphs

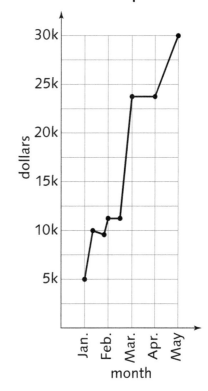

For use with Chapter 9, Question 9, section Grades 5–6: Data Analysis.
From *Good Questions for Math Teaching, Grades 5–8, Second Edition*, by Lainie Schuster and Nancy Anderson. Portsmouth, NH: Heinemann. © 2020 by Heinemann. May be photocopied for classroom use.

Reproducible 24

Dart Board

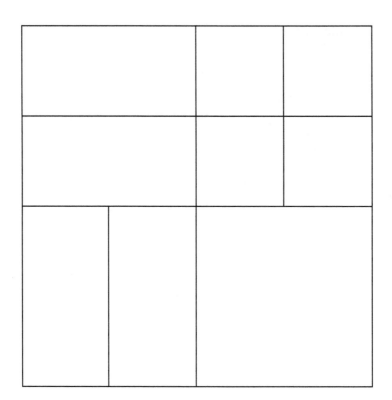

For use with Chapter 9, Question 2, section Grades 5–6: Probability.
From *Good Questions for Math Teaching, Grades 5–8, Second Edition*, by Lainie Schuster and Nancy Anderson. Portsmouth, NH: Heinemann. © 2020 by Heinemann. May be photocopied for classroom use.

REPRODUCIBLE 25

Bags of Marbles

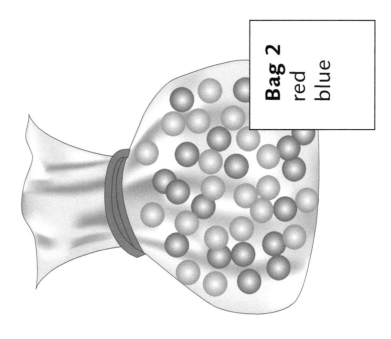

Bag 2
red
blue

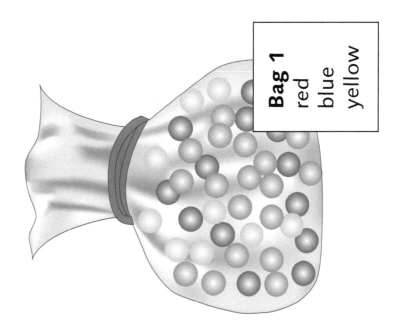

Bag 1
red
blue
yellow

For use with Chapter 9, Question 3, section Grades 5–6: Probability.
From *Good Questions for Math Teaching, Grades 5–8, Second Edition*, by Lainie Schuster and Nancy Anderson. Portsmouth, NH: Heinemann. © 2020 by Heinemann. May be photocopied for classroom use.

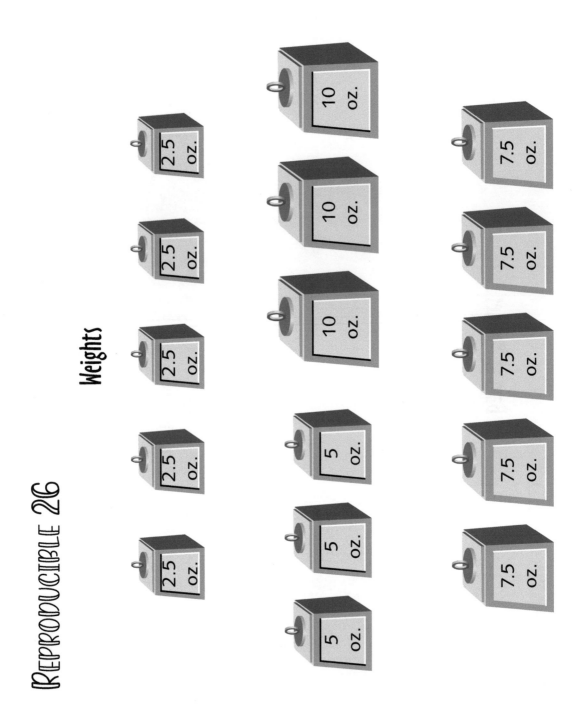

Weights

REPRODUCIBLE 26

For use with Chapter 10, Question 3, section Grades 5–6: Weight.
From *Good Questions for Math Teaching, Grades 5–8, Second Edition*, by Lainie Schuster and Nancy Anderson. Portsmouth, NH: Heinemann. © 2020 by Heinemann. May be photocopied for classroom use.

Reproducible 27

Irregular Polygon

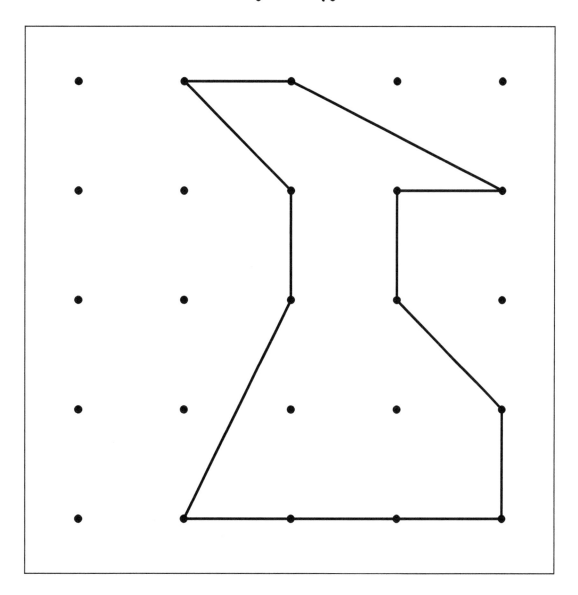

For use with Chapter 10, Question 8, section Grades 5–6: Area and Perimeter.
From *Good Questions for Math Teaching, Grades 5–8, Second Edition*, by Lainie Schuster and Nancy Anderson. Portsmouth, NH: Heinemann. © 2020 by Heinemann. May be photocopied for classroom use.

Reproducible 28

Cutout Polygon Models

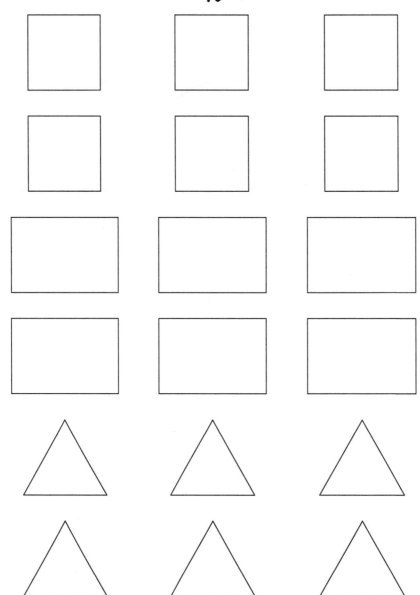

For use with Chapter 10, Question 15, section Grades 5–6: Area and Perimeter.
From *Good Questions for Math Teaching, Grades 5–8, Second Edition*, by Lainie Schuster and Nancy Anderson. Portsmouth, NH: Heinemann. © 2020 by Heinemann. May be photocopied for classroom use.

REPRODUCIBLE 29

Volume Pattern

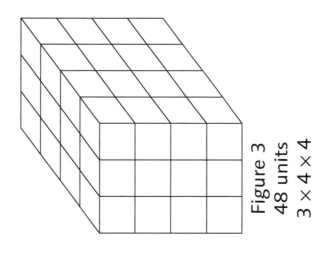

Figure 3
48 units
3 × 4 × 4

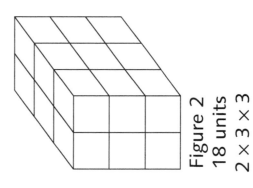

Figure 2
18 units
2 × 3 × 3

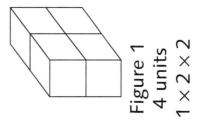

Figure 1
4 units
1 × 2 × 2

For use with Chapter 10, Question 1, section Grades 5–6: Volume.
From *Good Questions for Math Teaching, Grades 5–8, Second Edition*, by Lainie Schuster and Nancy Anderson. Portsmouth, NH: Heinemann. © 2020 by Heinemann. May be photocopied for classroom use.

Reproducible 30

Prisms

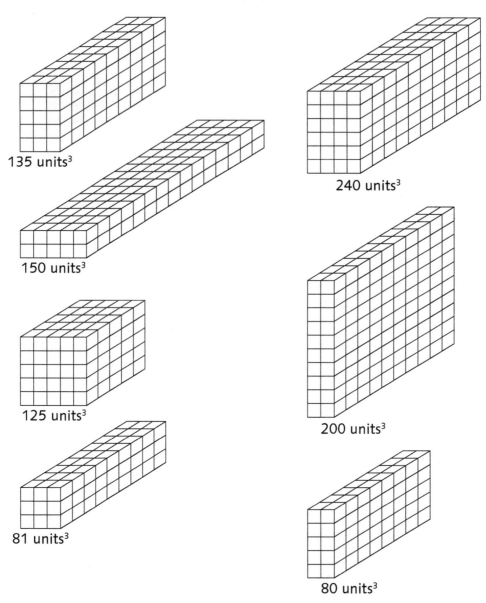

For use with Chapter 10, Question 6, section Grades 5–6: Volume.
From *Good Questions for Math Teaching, Grades 5–8, Second Edition*, by Lainie Schuster and Nancy Anderson. Portsmouth, NH: Heinemann. © 2020 by Heinemann. May be photocopied for classroom use.

Reproducible A

Graph Paper

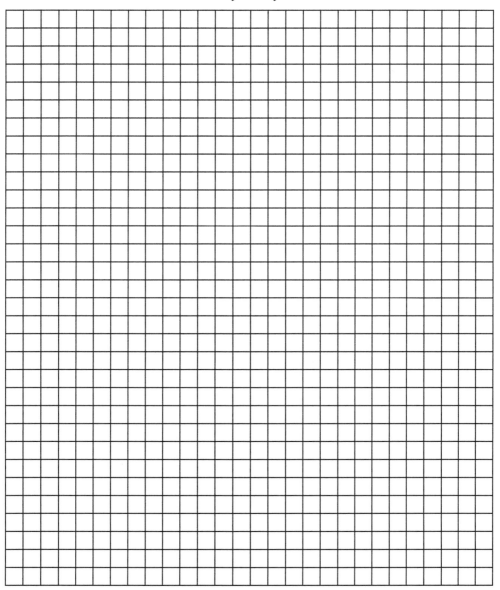

For use with multiple questions as you see fit.
From *Good Questions for Math Teaching, Grades 5–8, Second Edition*, by Lainie Schuster and Nancy Anderson. Portsmouth, NH: Heinemann. © 2020 by Heinemann. May be photocopied for classroom use.

Reproducible B

Dot Paper

For use with multiple questions as you see fit.
From *Good Questions for Math Teaching, Grades 5–8, Second Edition*, by Lainie Schuster and Nancy Anderson. Portsmouth, NH: Heinemann. © 2020 by Heinemann. May be photocopied for classroom use.

Reproducible C

Blank Spinner Faces

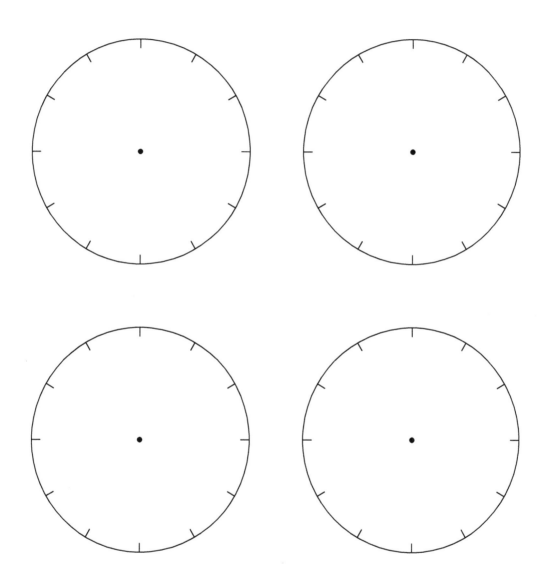

For use with multiple questions throughout Chapter 9.
From *Good Questions for Math Teaching, Grades 5–8, Second Edition*, by Lainie Schuster and Nancy Anderson. Portsmouth, NH: Heinemann. © 2020 by Heinemann. May be photocopied for classroom use.

References

Barnett-Clarke, Carne, William Fisher, Rick Marks, and Sharon Ross. 2010. *Developing Essential Understanding of Rational Numbers for Teaching Mathematics in Grades 3–5*. Essential Understanding Series. Reston, VA: National Council of Teachers of Mathematics.

Battista, Michael T., and Mary Berle-Carman. 1997. *Containers and Cubes: 3-D Geometry*. Investigations in Number, Data, and Space series. Glenview, IL: Scott Foresman.

Becker, Jerry P., and Shigeru Shimada. 1997. *The Open-Ended Approach: A New Proposal for Teaching Mathematics*. Reston, VA: National Council of Teachers of Mathematics.

Burns, Marilyn. 1992. *The Way to Math Solutions*. Sausalito, CA: Math Solutions.

———. 2015. *About Teaching Mathematics: A K–8 Resource*. 4th ed. Sausalito, CA: Math Solutions.

———. 2003. *The Fraction Kit*. Sausalito, CA: Math Solutions.

Chapin, Suzanne H. 1997. *Middle Grades Math*. Upper Saddle River, NJ: Prentice Hall.

Chapin, Suzanne H., and Art Johnson. 2006. *Math Matters: Understanding the Math You Teach, Grades K–8*. 2d ed. Sausalito, CA: Math Solutions.

Chapin, Suzanne H., Catherine O'Connor, and Nancy Canavan Anderson. 2013. *Talk Moves: A Teacher's Guide for Using Classroom Discussions in Math, Grades K–6*. 3d ed. Sausalito, CA: Math Solutions.

Christelow, Eileen. 1993. *The Five-Dog Night*. New York: Clarion Books.

Collins, John. 1992. *Developing Writing and Thinking Skills Across the Curriculum: A Practical Program for Schools*. West Newbury, MA: Collins Education.

Costa, Arthur L., and Bena Kallick, eds. 2000. *Activating and Engaging Habits of Mind*. Alexandria, VA: Association for Supervision and Curriculum Development.

Cuevas, Gilbert J., and Karol Yeatts. 2001. *Navigating Through Algebra in Grades 3–5*. Reston, VA: National Council of Teachers of Mathematics.

Dantonio, Marylou, and Paul C. Beisenherz. 2001. *Learning to Question, Questioning to Learn: Developing Effective Teacher Questioning Practices*. Needham Heights, MA: Allyn and Bacon.

Dodds, Dayle Anne. 2004. *Minnie's Diner: A Multiplying Menu*. Cambridge, MA: Candlewick Press.

Everyday Learning Corporation. 2002. *Everyday Mathematics: The University of Chicago School Mathematics Project*. Chicago: Everyday Learning.

Greenes, Carole, Linda Schulman Dacey, and Rika Spungin. 2001a. *Hot Math Topics, Grade 4: Estimation and Logical Reasoning*. Parsippany, NJ: Dale Seymour.

———. 2001b. *Hot Math Topics, Grade 4: Measurement and Geometry*. Parsippany, NJ: Dale Seymour.

———. 2001c. *Hot Math Topics, Grade 5: Algebraic Reasoning*. Parsippany, NJ: Dale Seymour.

———. 2001d. *Hot Math Topics, Grade 5: Fractions and Decimals*. Parsippany, NJ: Dale Seymour.

———. 2001e. *Hot Math Topics, Grade 5: Geometry and Measurement*. Parsippany, NJ: Dale Seymour.

Lappan, Glenda, James Fey, William Fitzgerald, Susan Friel, and Elizabeth Phillips. 2002a. *Connected Mathematics Project: Bits and Pieces I*. Glenview, IL: Prentice Hall.

———. 2002b. *Connected Mathematics Project: Bits and Pieces II*. Glenview, IL: Prentice Hall.

———. 2002c. *Connected Mathematics Project: Comparing and Scaling*. Glenview, IL: Prentice Hall.

———. 2002d. *Connected Mathematics Project: Covering and Surrounding*. Glenview, IL: Prentice Hall.

———. 2002e. *Connected Mathematics Project: Filling and Wrapping*. Glenview, IL: Prentice Hall.

———. 2002f. *Connected Mathematics Project: How Likely Is It?* Glenview, IL: Prentice Hall.

———. 2002g. *Connected Mathematics Project: Moving Straight Ahead*. Glenview, IL: Prentice Hall.

———. 2002h. *Connected Mathematics Project: Prime Time*. Glenview, IL: Prentice Hall.

———. 2002i. *Connected Mathematics Project: Shapes and Designs*. Glenview, IL: Prentice Hall.

———. 2002j. *Connected Mathematics Project: Stretching and Shrinking*. Glenview, IL: Prentice Hall.

Lobato, Joanne, and Amy Ellis. 2010. *Developing Essential Understanding of Ratios, Proportions, and Proportional Reasoning for Teaching Mathematics in Grades 6–8*. Essential Understanding Series. Reston, VA: National Council of Teachers of Mathematics.

McNamara, Julie. 2015. *Beyond Invert and Multiply: Making Sense of Fraction Computation*. Sausalito, CA: Math Solutions.

National Council of Teachers of Mathematics (NCTM). 2000. *Principles and Standards for School Mathematics*. Reston, VA: Author.

National Governors Association Center for Best Practices and the Council of State School Officers. 2019. *Common Core State Standards Initiative: Common Core State Standards for Mathematics*, www.corestandards.org /Math/Practice.

Schuster, Lainie. 2010. *Enriching Your Math Curriculum, Grade 5: A Month-to-Month Resource*. Sausalito, CA: Math Solutions.

Sullivan, Peter, and Pat Lilburn. 2002. *Good Questions for Math Teaching: Why Ask Them and What to Ask, K–6*. Sausalito, CA: Math Solutions.

Wickett, MaryAnn, and Marilyn Burns. 2001. *Teaching Arithmetic: Lessons for Extending Multiplication, Grades 4–5*. Sausalito, CA: Math Solutions.

Wickett, Mary Ann, Katherine Kharas, and Marilyn Burns. 2002. *Lessons for Algebraic Thinking, Grades 3–5*. Sausalito, CA: Math Solutions.

Math Solutions Publications is now part of Heinemann. To learn more about our resources and authors please visit www.Heinemann.com/Math.